Enlightenment,

Not What I Expected.

By: Karl R. Emde

My experiences living with and learning from a Swami on his ashram in India.
July 12, 2006 to April 15, 2007

This work depicts actual events in the life of the author as truthfully as recollection permits. Occasionally, dialogue consistent with the character or nature of the person speaking has been supplemented. All persons within are actual individuals; there are no composite characters. The names of all individuals have been changed to respect their privacy.

ISBN: 978-1-7777027-1-7 (paper back)
ISBN: 978-1-7777027-0-0 (epub)

Dedication

This book is dedicated to my Mother who instilled in me the desire to follow my heart and view the world as an opportunity for growth. She also introduced me to Swami.

I also dedicate this book to my incredibly supportive family. My wife who saw the initial changes in me and trusted enough to support my quest, and our two sons who helped take care of liquidating a lifetime to support my journey

Introduction

As a teenager, I devoured anything metaphysical. Life was a challenge to fit into. What fascinated me was a foreign taboo to most people I knew. While I did what most teenagers do at that time in my life, I spent a lot of my free time reading books I could not discuss with my friends. A book I read about an Indian guru sparked a yearning in me to be personally trained by such a person. Little did I know that it wouldn't be until my late 40s that circumstances would conspire to make the experience possible.

This book is a chronological recounting of my intense day-to-day experiences, emotional ups and downs and spiritual experiences life on an ashram for nine months can evoke.

My goal in sharing this part of my life with you is primarily to spark within you a desire to find your own spiritual path to enlightenment.

Secondly, if a visit to an Indian ashram is in your future, this recounting of my journey will hopefully give you a small taste of what that experience might be like for you and the role a guru can play in that experience.

I am forever grateful for the discoveries my guru helped me uncover. Although difficult at the time, I have no regrets about my time in India. My life now is infinitely more blissful with a solid foundation of peace within. I bless all who read these pages with a more bliss-filled life and an ever-expanding peace of mind.

Blissfully yours,
Karl R. Emde

Table of Contents

Chapter 1

Finding My Peace

White dots of light shot at the windshield of my Jeep like I was traveling through an interstellar wormhole, making the highway over the mountain pass slippery and icy, yet I felt safe and protected. The synchronicity of powers beyond my control or understanding coordinated my life events to lead me to this weekend meditation workshop. Once I decided to attend the workshop, circumstances fell into place so effortlessly, I knew I was guided. Life was answering my pleas for purpose. The purpose of this workshop may still be a mystery, but there was no doubt about where I was meant to be.

I had been invited to a weekend meditation workshop presented by a genuine enlightened swami from India. To just be in the presence of an enlightened being is enough to release sub-conscious issues that might otherwise take a lifetime of unguided work to resolve.

From my earliest memories, I knew I was profoundly more powerful than I was taught. Growing up, I read many metaphysical books and attended classes and training sessions to expand the depth and breadth of my understanding of life on earth. This meditation workshop was one more attempt to fill the aching void in my knowledge.

I caught a flash of colored light out the corner of my eye. I was thinking metaphysical, and this light felt very physical. It was just for a moment. I couldn't see it anywhere on the road ahead or behind now. As the long, slow corner of the highway straightened out, the light caught my eye again. It was a police car far behind me, barely visible in the dark and blowing snow. I checked on the police car in my mirror from time to time, but the lights were not catching up very fast. I checked my speed; it was plus or minus a little as usual, nothing to worry about. I continued with my metaphysical musings, expecting the policeman to pass me at some point. The car didn't appear to be catching up at all now. I all but forgot about him until quite sometime later, and I realized the car was directly behind me. I didn't understand why he didn't just pass. There were two lanes and nobody else in sight. Then it dawned on me: he wanted me to pull over. When I am not grounded, thinking about esoteric things like swamis and meditating, the most apparent connections aren't spontaneous. It took a while to stop the Jeep on the icy road. When the officer finally got to my window, he asked me if I knew how fast I was going. Of course, I did. I checked when I saw him approaching. I told him, "The speed I usually travel." He told me the speed limits were for ideal driving conditions, and I needed to slow down. I didn't say to him that my guardian angels were escorting me and wouldn't let anything happen because I had an important date with the rest of my life. Although, when the officer asked where I was going in such a hurry, I did explain about the meditation workshop. He kindly let me off with a warning. I thanked the officer and my angels for saving me the expense of a ticket. The six hours of driving to the workshop felt like a comfortable drive home after work.

I arrived without further incident at the free Friday night introductory session in a strip mall of professional buildings. The room was wide open with beautiful luxurious red patterned carpet. At one end of the room, a small altar was set up with a cardboard cut-out likeness of the swami adorned with beautiful flower garlands. Little brass containers surrounded the picture. There were flowers, lit wicks lying in oil, and chairs facing the altar. A table with an elegant sari as a tablecloth was being set up by volunteers along the back of the room with CDs, malas, pictures, and other swami merchandise beside a couple of empty tables. The atmosphere felt friendly and comfortable.

When our speaker introduced himself, about twenty of us listened to him explain how he had met a guru in India who profoundly inspired him. This guru so inspired Aarav, he moved to the guru's ashram in India and participated in many of his teachings and had deeply blissful spiritual experiences with the guru's guidance. Spreading his guru's knowledge and enlightenment was now Aarav's spiritual training.

This workshop was one of Aarav's first times teaching what he had learned. He started by explaining what Chakras, energy centers in our bodies were and how we could exert more control over our lives by learning how to control the energy movements in our bodies. Below is a very abridged version of his list of our energy centers and how to manage them.

Root Chakra - base of spine (Muladahara).
  Locked by fantasy and imagination.
  Unlocked by living in the moment.
Sacral - two inches below navel (Swadhishtana).
  Locked by fear, especially of death.
  Unlocked by acceptance of fear.
Solar Plexus - navel (Manipura).
  Locked when you worry.
  Unlocked when you stop worrying.
Heart Chakra - center of chest (Anahata).
  Locked when seeking attention.
  Unlocked when expressing unconditional love.
Throat Chakra - throat (Vishuddhi).
  Locked by comparison and jealousy.
  Unlocked by being who we are without concern.
Third Eye Chakra - between eyebrows (Ajna).
  Locked by seriousness and ego.

Unlocked by shedding all forms of ego.

Crown Chakra - top of head (Sahasara).

Locked by discontentment.

Unlocked with gratitude and contentment.

Aarav guided us through a mesmerizing heart chakra activation meditation. We moved our chairs to form a circle. Aarav started us humming through our noses as loudly and for as long as we could with each breath. He directed our attention to the sensation in our chests created by the vibration of our humming. The sound of us humming in unison was blissfully uplifting. My inner voice was silenced. My attention was so focused on creating the humming sound, hearing the humming, and feeling the vibration that I forgot to listen to that little insistent voice in my head. All of us humming together was so loud, I was sure the sound was audible outside the building. It was exhilarating. At the twenty-minute mark, Aarav said, STOP! There was an intensely deep silence. Our chests were still vibrating. I could feel the ebbing sound waves pulling tension from me.

The silence was not the absence of sound, but the awareness of a profound sense of peace residing deep within us. Once revealed, this peace is accessible any time we choose to take the time to focus on it; it is an intense connection with something so much deeper than I was ever aware of before. I was thankful beyond measure. The feeling and connection with that peace remain with me to this day. I mark this experience as the beginning of my path to enlightenment. Hooked with that one little taste, I was up for whatever the rest of the weekend might bring.

On Saturday, Aarav led us through three different meditations and exercises, one for each of three more chakras with information and sharing sessions with each one. The empty tables along the back wall turned into a bountiful buffet of very delicious vegetarian Indian food at lunch and supper time. On Sunday, we were given information and meditations for the remaining three chakras.

I had taken the first step and was now firmly on my path to enlightenment. Later I would learn that I was much further along than one step. Just being aware that there were conscious steps to take was the beginning. Seeing and being open to the synchronicities of life is the real beginning. Regardless of the number of this step, I felt I was answering my soul's call.

After that inspirational weekend, my search for more spiritual information became even more obsessive. I meditated each morning consistently, revisiting my core of profound peace. Sometimes, the peace came quickly, and other times, not at all. In April, I discovered that Aarav's Indian guru was coming to Canada to give the next level of the meditation program himself. I registered immediately and couldn't wait to experience what might happen next.

The next level meeting was in a much larger hall. The energy from the Indian swami at this workshop was much more potent. At the first meditation workshop, my feelings were warm and comfortable, like a meeting of old friends getting reacquainted. This new workshop was beyond another level of intensity. I could feel the light I had cultivated in the center of my chest expanding and expanding like a meditation with my eyes open. The overwhelming compulsion to attend this workshop was satisfied before it even started.

Deep in my inner being, I knew attending this workshop had been meticulously coordinated at my soul level, probably long before I was born. I didn't have any choice. Drifting aimlessly in my spiritual search for a deeper meaning to life was over. I had crossed the threshold of that open subconscious door and was now comfortably feeling it close my life of searching behind me.

At the entrance to the meeting hall, I saw a sign above the biggest pile of shoes I had ever seen that read, "Leave your shoes and your worries here. Take your shoes at the end!" There was loud devotional music playing, and many volunteers were carefully coordinating all the details of this well-planned and executed event. The large meeting room was half-filled with over 400 people. The other half of the hall filled with tables laden with all manner of spiritual merchandise from Rudraksha beaded necklaces, bracelets, meditation CDs, blessed items, brass deities, and the guru's many books. I was a little overwhelmed by the industry of it all.

Most participants sat on the carpeted floor. A few experienced followers up at the front had a plethora of pillows, blankets, and even legless beach chairs. The blissful energy in the room made meditation easy. Swami finally made his entrance with a wide inviting smile. The buzzing energy in the room shifted noticeably into a calmer, more peaceful energy. It felt warm and safe, like everybody in that room was family. Tears ran down my face as I embraced a deep appreciation and respect for the complexity of the coordination the Universe undertook to bring all our little lives together in such a momentous way so we could all be together at this moment to share this collective experience. I understood that people and their higher selves do not coordinate their lives; the vibration of their being emanates into the world attracting events and people who harmonize with their frequency. In other words, we unconsciously moved heaven and earth to answer this call. When Swami spoke, his voice carried right through me. He was hypnotic.

It took me a while to get past this guru's thick Indian accent and cultural idiosyncrasies. I was concentrating so hard on understanding his words, I almost missed his message. At that moment of my realization, Swami told us his words were a distraction to keep our minds busy so he could work on our subconscious. I was stunned. It was like he was talking directly to me. I felt more connected with this guy the more he spoke. My heart center was vibrating and expanding. Meditations at home to visualize and incrementally expand my heart chakra exploded to the size of a basketball, and I wasn't even meditating. My heart was overflowing with bliss. There was no doubt that I was exactly where I was meant to be.

At the end of the first day, I got my first energy transmission, called darshan. I knelt in front of the guru. He placed his right thumb on my third eye. The sensation was like love pouring out of swami's thumb into my body. I was in bliss. The love poured into my third eye, through my head, and down my neck. When the flow of love passed my throat chakra, I took a breath. As soon as I took that breath, the flow stopped. Swami looked into my eyes and smiled. I was a devotee. Volunteers whisked me away to make way for the next participant. Note to self: take a deeper breath before the next darshan!

There were many guided meditations that weekend. All were effortless and intense compared to meditating on my own. My usual mind chatter just wasn't there. Inner silence was my new normal. At the end of the weekend, the guru told all four hundred of us he would initiate anybody interested in being a healer. I was intrigued, but reluctant, as healing is a big responsibility. I was not interested in the business of healing. Still, the people around me convinced me that it was improbable an opportunity like this would come up again in my life, and the fact that the Universe had arranged for me to be here at this time was a gift to be taken seriously.

I stayed behind, the program ended, and I gratefully accepted Swami's offer to be initiated. There were about forty of us waiting expectantly after all the other participants departed. We helped the volunteers pack up all the merchandise. I questioned the volunteers who had experienced the initiation to understand a healer's job description. I was nervous but genuinely seeking a higher expression of myself—a me free of societal programming. A me who could see the mirror that each person holds up for me and honor the lesson they are offering.

Swami came back into the room, and everyone fell silent. We were all excited and nervous at the same time. Swami sat quietly, and we gathered on the floor at his feet expectantly. He explained how Chakras worked, how they looked like little spinning vortexes attached at the small end to energy points in our body, and how there are seven of them from our root chakra at the base of our spine to the crown chakra at the top of our head. The new information for me was that when we move our consciousness from wakefulness to sleep, our chakras also retract from the perceived world into one internal chakra in the center of our chest called the Ananda-Ghanda to regenerate. They close up and become dormant while our consciousness moves into higher dimensions in the sleep state. The healing initiation was accomplished by Swami opening our Ananda Ghanda center and metaphorically throwing away the door, opening our Ananda Ghanda center for all time. He told us our lives would never be the same after this opening because the barrier between wakefulness and meditation would be gone. We would be in a state of constant meditation. When asked how anybody could function in the world in such a state, he simply said, "Like me!" His center is open, and he functions perfectly well.

We all accepted his reassurances and lined up for the initiation. The reality of a constant state of meditation is that the depth and intensity of meditation is directly proportional to your level of concentration. Only when you consciously focus inward do you realize your connection to the peace within. The initiation involved Swami putting his right thumb on our third eye, like a darshan, but while he held his thumb there, he waved his left hand over our chest like he was shooing flies away from our solar plexus. Some of us took more "shooing" than others!

When my turn came, I remembered my previous darshan experience and took a deeper breath in preparation for an extended energetic experience. With eyes closed, I was surprised not to feel any energy pouring into my third eye, but I soon energetically felt his "shooing" motions over my chest like the pounding bass of massive speakers in a rock concert. Each swish felt like a massive darshan directed at my chest. After three swishes, he was finished, and I was in bliss. I felt like I floated back to where I was sitting on the floor and fell into deep and soulful meditation without even trying.

When we were all initiated, he told us that the initiation experience was just a taste of what was open to us if we would come to his ashram in India. There were many questions by everyone there about his offer. My heart had already made the decision. In the end, twenty-seven of us told him we wanted to experience life on his ashram in India. We were required to make a formal request in the form of a letter and a resume. Swami would review the letters and make a decision based on each case.

It took a couple of months to be granted acceptance. I made arrangements for leave from my teaching job. I got my visa application and my first passport. A couple of months later, I arrived in India at Swami's ashram to find that only a few of us had followed through and made the trip to his ashram that was unprepared for international guests.

Life before my Ananda Ghanda opening and after is profoundly different. Before the opening, bliss was unpredictably limited to meditations, where I focused hard and deep enough to attain a sufficient level of detachment. Now, all I have to do is relax a bit and drop my focus from whatever is around me and focus inward to feel waves of bliss washing over me. If I close my eyes, even for a moment, I am aware that I am in a light meditative state and can more easily quiet my mind. When I intentionally meditate now, it is easier to quiet my mind and to find my inner peace, my happy place. Waiting in my car at a traffic light, waiting in line at the grocery store, or just about anywhere, I can close my eyes for a moment and disconnect from what is around me. I am eternally grateful to Swami for showing me this path to peace.

Chapter 2

Finding My Place

After the first workshop in Canada, my daily meditations became better and better. By better meditations, I mean, my mind chatter was easier to detach from. After the second workshop, I realized that a state of detached meditation is a normal human experience, and intense emotional responses are the object of study and discovery to overcome its triggers. I learned that my mind would no more shut up than my heart would stop beating. I understood why some meditation methods helped me find peace more easily. My mind had its job to do, and my meditation had its purpose.

Meditation is not about quieting the mind. It is about being able to see the thoughts floating by in your mind's eye and not getting caught up in them. Detaching from thoughts is like watching leaves floating down a stream—not noticing the color of the leaves or what tree they may have come from and merely allowing the thoughts to form, rise up, and float off into space without paying attention to them. When your attention focuses on a thought, you give it energy. When you provide it with energy, the law of attraction kicks in, and other associated thoughts are magnetized to your attention. Just relax your attention again and let the cluster of thoughts go. A trick to let thoughts go that worked for me is to take a deep, deep breath and immediately relax my whole body, allowing the air to flow out without effort naturally. For ten or thirty seconds or so, my body does not require an in-breath. In those few seconds, I found I could relax more deeply than at any other time without needing to breathe.

In those moments of deep relaxation, I can detach from thoughts most easily. As I slowly return to my normal rhythm of breathing, I can more easily remain in my detached state and completely disconnect from my mind chatter. I am far from masterful, but I feel confident that I am on the right path.

In anticipation of my new life in India, I was overly optimistic, having never traveled before. I was mentally prepared to spend the rest of my life in India pursuing ever-expanding levels of enlightenment. Reality couldn't have been more different. When I arrived in India, I felt compelled to record my experiences to be able to share them with family. Initially, I recorded my experiences on whatever scraps of paper I could find. When I had time, I emailed them to my wife, Lynn, who forwarded them to family and, unknown to me at the time, some Swami devotees in Vancouver. Presented here are my experiences in India as I recorded them in my emails to Lynn with some editing for readability.

Dear Lynn,

While I was comfortably sitting, reading my book, waiting to board my flight to India, a frazzled-looking middle-aged woman with way too many packages and a high-energy, out-of-control young son came into the waiting area. She was clearly in need of some organizational and child-rearing skills. There was something about her son appearing to be in control and her apparent inability to manage all her packages that was mirroring something in my life I needed to reflect on. I loved that she appeared very relaxed about her situation. Her son was inquisitive and fearless, sure signs of being raised in a supportive and loving environment. The relationship between this mother and son was beautiful, even if the boy was running around with little respect for other people. In spite of my assessment, this woman and her son were still pushing my buttons. I enjoyed the challenge of being an observer but wasn't seeing my lesson in this situation yet. As fate would have it, we ended up sitting beside each other with her son in the seat between us on the long first leg of my flight. My lesson came into pretty sharp focus when we were in closer proximity. I did my best to turn off my teacher training and to let go of the need to control the situation and think there was anything I could teach this woman. She was happy with her life, and what could be more beautiful than that? Her son and I enjoyed each other's company. She unknowingly showed me how to be unconditionally happy.

In Singapore, I signed up for a city bus tour. I will never take car ownership in Canada for granted again. Aside from the heat and humidity, Singapore is a beautiful European-like, well-laid-out city. Singapore was only formed 200 years ago, occupied by both Japan and Britain. It is now one of the wealthiest countries in the world. I never really appreciated the amount of undeveloped land available in Canada until this tour of Singapore.

I found the only hotel computer for public use in the lobby connected to the internet to send this message. I have been told the Ashram in India is somewhat rural, and the internet may not be reliable, so I'll connect while I can. The hotel here is beautiful, very expensive looking, with marble everything and very high ceilings. The plumbing is different; I'll spare you the details, but it would not pass Canadian code. The floor tiles in the hotel room are a half-inch higher than in the bathroom. I painfully stubbed my toe on the ledge the first time exiting the bathroom. I don't know if this is an accident or an intentional design.

Thinking of you often!

Love,

Karl

Any situation in my life that generates emotion is showing me an unconscious emotional attachment that needs to be resolved. This attachment will reoccur and reoccur until I understand what initiated that attachment. With understanding, attachments vaporize. The situations that once caused that emotion will continue to happen, but they will no longer trigger the emotional response it once did. When I meditate, I learn to recognize how energy moves in my body. When I get triggered, I acknowledge and feel the energy building moments before my ego labels it anything like anger. In that moment of detached energy buildup, I have an opportunity to witness other emotional connections to past events in my life where the energy felt the same. The witnessing of those past emotional experiences, connected to the present emotionally triggering experience, reveals the ego's unconscious connection. In light of the unconscious emotional connection, the trigger vaporizes.

Chapter 3

So This Is an Ashram

Dear Lynn

I am in the town nearest the ashram, actually a village. It is small by Indian standards, with only a million or so people. The village is called Bidadi, located a half-hour southwest of Bangalore and 15 minutes by auto-rickshaw from the ashram. I have about 20min before the taxi takes us ashramites to Swami's discourse in a sizeable two-level theatre in Bangalore. A power blackout sent my first attempt at this email into the digital abyss. I learned something new today: power blackouts are brownouts if planned. Each computer has a UPS, but something was wrong with this one. A schedule posted on the computer would have been useful. There is not enough power for the whole city, so they have district blackouts in rotation for predetermined lengths of time.

It’s the second day at the ashram and I'm already off to Swami's discourse in Bangalore. The ashram is only a few years old and still setting up its infrastructure. The internet is always on the pending list.

When I arrived at Bangalore Airport a week ago, I was surprised and overwhelmed by the smell. I thought the smell was the airport service people cleaning out the airplane toilet holding tanks. In Canada, I would have just held my breath and walked to fresher air. No, this foul smell of burning garbage and human waste is the standard air quality here. You get used to it. I suspect the air quality was also adversely affected by the many homeless people outside the large glass waiting room windows lying against the airport walls and windows. The airport was dirty and littered with garbage by Western standards. It looked like the airport was still under construction. Wires were hanging from other wires, T-Bar ceilings were not finished, and there was a severe lack of signage. Construction in many areas must have appeared to have reached the point of being functional, so they were never completed. I was in culture shock. Baggage felt like it took way too long to get to the airport baggage handling system. When my bags finally rolled in on the conveyor, I almost had to fight a porter to collect my baggage. The porter tried to pull my bags off the conveyor all the time saying, "I help, I help, I help," with me saying "No, no, no." I had to physically pull my bags from his hands. This is where being 6'6" and 270lbs helps when asserting myself. Even after wresting my bags out of the porter's hands and putting my baggage onto the trolly cart, he still demanded payment. I couldn't believe him. I kept saying no, but he kept following me. He continued to follow me right out of the terminal onto the sidewalk out front.

Once outside, I was overwhelmed by new smells and a whole new culture of driving. The smells of burning garbage and sewage were even stronger. I finally relented and asked the porter to find me a taxi. When he returned with a cab, I gave him two hundred rupees, to which he replied, "five hundred rupees." I gave him another one hundred rupees and got in the taxi. My plane arrival was too early in the morning to expect any kind of reception at any ashram. I spent the night at a charming back street hotel recommended by the taxi driver. Incidentally, the tiling being lower in the bathroom was the same as the hotel in Singapore. I have to assume this method of tiling is intentional. Breakfast was served on the rooftop. The building was only a few stories, but taller than the surrounding buildings. The smell was much better at the hotel. There were some beautiful big trees filled with beautifully colored birds and a few monkeys. I was the only one having breakfast, so the service was fast, and the fruit juice was fresh squeezed.

Traffic in India is a little intense for me. The taxi driver assured me there are stringent traffic rules. The most important one being the vehicle ahead of you has the right of way. Regular honking is required to warn other drivers and pedestrians of your presence. Once you learn to detach from any illusion of control, traffic here can be quite entertaining. There is that control issue popping up again!

The first day at the ashram, the taxi dropped me off in a large dusty dirt parking lot full of cars in front of a large arched building about ninety feet wide by a hundred and fifty feet long. I had arrived in the middle of huge celebrations, with lots of people attending a swami discourse and a couple of weddings with no room for me. Nobody I talked to knew I was coming, even with a copy of my letter of permission. The few ashram staff I found were overwhelmed by all the event participants. I was on my own to find my way around. No reception for newcomers was this ashram's policy and the beginning of one's spiritual training.

I walked around freely, exploring the entire ashram. The only place that was off-limits and always remained so was Swami's modest personal house. The ashram itself is pretty crude with little infrastructure. Sewage from toilets and kitchen run in open ditches. Wiring is strung from one building to the next and doubles as a clothesline. Swami's house looks beautiful and well finished. It sits off in a fenced-off corner of the ashram.

The meeting hall (Ananda Saba) is the central building where all events take place. The floor is smooth concrete, and the trusses inside are hidden with white sheets, but the toilets are a short walk away across a bridge over one of the sewage ditches. There are only six toilets for each gender. When there are events, the lineups for toilets are long. The reception room at the front of the Ananda Saba is way too small for the number of people that are processed for events. The kitchen only accommodates a few cooks at once and is not designed to serve hundreds of people, but somehow they do. Three small round eating huts are enough for the few ashramites and workers that live here full time.

There are a few rooms set up motel-like in an "L" shape for ashramites. Down the hill, there is a building of eight rooms for guests called the Eight Room Block, where each room squeezes in three bunk beds and an ensuite. Another smaller building, called the Gate

House, houses the only internet connection and a library with a publishing room at the back and an adjoining room for administration. There is an amazing massive banyan tree that is said to be six hundred years old. The best part is the laughing temple. It is eight feet round with a grass roof and is Swami's favorite place to hang out. When Swami is seated in the laughing temple, he looks out over a meager but well-tended flower garden. It is called the laughing temple because of Swami's often heard, loud, distinctive, and infectious laugh. Swami is open to just about anybody any time of the day in his little laughing temple.

Fortunately, the celebrations included an all-night meditation that I was allowed to attend. It started at 5:00 pm and went until 5:00 am the next morning. I registered and was excited to be getting an early start on my enlightenment until I realized the program was in Tamil. I didn't care; I was where I needed to be. Shoes and socks have to be removed before going into any ashram building. I left my footwear outside and my bag in the reception room and found an empty seat in the back of the sizeable wall-to-wall audience. Swami looked me square in the eye and spoke directly to me in English. "Those who do not speak Hindi are perfect for this discourse because they know they do not understand and will be able to feel the energies. Those who think they understand will miss the energy when they try to focus on my words."

The energy of all those people meditating was limitless. When I went up for the energy darshan at the end, Swami said to me, "I know you!" with his charismatic smile. I agreed! A part of me had come home. Even though I had no accommodation, I felt everything was exactly as it should be. Nobody questioned my being there, and I was free to walk around and get an idea of where everything and everybody was during meal times.

I got a bunk in a semi-private room. Semi-private means only three bunk beds in a tiny room instead of a bunk bed in a forty-bed bunkhouse. My new room had the added luxury of an indoor washroom. There were only two guys in the room already, so we each got a bunk bed. The door was secured by a deadbolt that could only be operated from the outside. I later learned that doors secured like this are typical in this area of India. Some mechanisms include a handle that can operate the slide bolt from the inside.

The second day was much quieter after all the weekend attendees left. The ashram's population fell from hundreds to twenty-something. Registration lineups went down to zero, and office staff finally had a break. I attempted to register for the year-long program. The year-long program was so new it didn't have a name yet. The office staff didn't know how to process my request. While they investigated, I was sent to the banyan tree to meditate.

The banyan tree was only a couple hundred yards up the road through a farmer's field. As I approached the banyan tree, I was transfixed, in awe of the massive tree's size and energy. I had never seen anything like it. Thick gravity-defying branches reached out so far they needed their own tree trunks. The tree was like a forest unto itself with a canopy as big as a house. The ground under the tree was well-tended and swept clean. A large deity sat on a built-up mound of rock and concrete with a likeness of a large snake wrapped around the bottom.

I must have been standing there for a while because I was shocked back to the present by a sweet young voice saying, "Hi, Karl." The voice was from a fellow Vancouverite. I was so thankful for a fellow English-speaking Canadian. We quickly became good friends.

I soon learned that the banyan tree is where everybody is sent as the ashram's unofficial waiting room. Later, access to this beautiful tree would be restricted to preserve its energy. My friend had only arrived a few days earlier but was a big help in getting adjusted and oriented.

The well water on this ashram is exceptionally pure and clean by Indian standards; however, "Westerners" still need to go to the kitchen for boiled and filtered water.

I am currently on the second night of a three-day discourse in Bangalore. It cost us 500r for all three days, $12.50Cd, including food. The ashram program I chose is called Ananda Yogum. Participants are called yogis. Payment is in the form of labor around the ashram. Swami says I should have no trouble reaching enlightenment in one year. Apparently, enlightenment can be achieved in twelve days if you are intense enough. It is all about intensity. He gave us free access to his library, and we are to read a selection of his books. As a yogi, Swami will teach us the two programs I took in Canada and the healer's initiation again the Indian way, which means more intensity and more time.

Got to go, my fellow internationals are trying to drag me away from this computer in the hotel lobby to get food with them and then to the other end of the block where the discourse is.

Love,
Karl

Early days at the ashram were blissful and relaxing. Memories of my relentlessly busy life as a Canadian high school teacher were fading fast like a bad dream as I easily immersed myself in this new life. There were no bells or hard and fast deadlines. New arrivals decompressed from their previous lives on their own schedules. I slept more than I expected. It was all part of the adjustment. The few issues I had about the ashram and how things operated were nothing compared to my pre-ashram life. I was not looking back, opening my life up to new possibilities. I was in heaven.

Dear Lynn,

> When I meditated back home in Canada about what life might be like in this ashram here in India, I would inexplicably see a big snake. I know snakes mean something else in dreams, but in a place of higher aspirations, how could such a big snake invade my meditations? When I walked up to the banyan tree for the first time, I almost laughed out loud. A four-foot-high statue of a deity sits on a three-foot-high mound of cemented rock. At the base of the mound is a

big concrete snake that encircles the mound. I found out that the concrete snake is a tribute to an actual snake that lives near the tree about 15 feet long. I can see it's slither marks in the sand if I am early enough in the morning. That has surely got to be a sign I am not here by accident.

Love,

Karl

Chapter 4

Slowing to a New Rhythm

Dear Lynn,

Last night a lady whom I was told is a famous Indian actress told us about an incident two years ago when all the ashramites were walking up to the banyan tree very early in the morning. It was still twilight. Three straggling ashramites heard footsteps behind them and became afraid, so they hurried up to the safety of the group already at the banyan tree. Even further behind the three stragglers, another ashramite did not recognize the person or his dress walking ahead of him, so he sketched a likeness of him when he got to the banyan tree. After Puja, Swami was sitting quietly on his porch meditating. He heard footsteps nearby. No one is allowed inside his personal yard without permission. He hadn't given permission for anyone to be there, so when he judged the intruder to be in the right position, he opened his eyes and pounced on the guy, grabbing him by the ankle. Swami looked up to see who he had caught and was shocked to discover that it was a perfect likeness of Shiva. Swami released his ankle and stood up just in time to see him walk around behind a big rock near his house. Swami ran after him, but he was gone. Later that evening, the artist consulted Swami about the strange person he had seen walking up to the banyan tree and showed Swami the sketch. Now there was no doubt. It was Shiva. How anyone would know what Shiva looks like is a study in itself.

The last few weeks have been, as Swami says, "intense." The only free time I have had has been early in the morning or late at night. After the Bhakti Spurana Program (BSP), we had three days off, but it took us all three days to clean the meeting hall.

At the end of the BSP, some young ashramites got into a bucket of white flour-like powder and started throwing it at everybody like Divali. It turns out the powder was special ceremonial ash called vibhuti—the same ash that Swami wipes on his forehead. One of the participants told me it's a blessing to wear the ash, which is often mixed with drinks to heal digestion issues. Drying and then burning sacred cow dung is how to make vibhuti. On this ashram, it is made by burning sacred banyan tree leaves, thank goodness! But the mess still pushed every keep-clean button I have! Today, there is another BSP in Tamil, no internationals. No internationals is why I have a bit of free time. I hope they keep the kids out of the vibhuti this time.

I participated in the Guru Bakthi Program (all night meditation), Swami's discourse in Bangalore, Saptha Yogam (4 days in Salem, 8 hours en route), a four-day Indian NSP, a four-day Indian BSP, and a two-day Indian Healers Initiation Training. I am concurrently enrolled in the one-year Ananda Yogam Program. With all these courses and training, I should be a wink away from enlightenment.

I have been to Bangalore a couple of times and Bidadi for fruit. We get a few people together and share the cost of the taxi. Bidadi costs about 150 rupees in a three-wheeled auto-rickshaw. Divided by three, it is about a dollar there and back. A trip to Bangalore is 1400 rupees or about $10.00. In Bangalore, Brigade Street is popular with Westerners with familiar stores like a coffee bar that makes a great caramel frappe, a Western-style grocery store, and a five-story mall at the bottom of the street. Best of all, my Canadian debit card works there, but the ashram provides everything I need.

Four more people arrived the day before yesterday for the one-year Ananda Yogam Program from the Caribbean. We now have eight international people.

Love,
Karl

The early days at the ashram were blissful. I had no idea what an ashram was before being invited here. Now I live in one. I loved the freedom to work only for my enlightenment. In everything we did, we were mindful of how our enlightenment was being affected. We were called their "international batch," and also "the outside inmates." We helped each other adapt to cultural differences, such as gender segregation and a general lack of privacy. As a diverse group of International men and women from the US, Caribbean, and Canada, our issues and perspectives were taken more seriously in the ashram's attempts to attract more international visitors. The ashram was only about three years old at this point. We were as much a resource of information for them as Swami was a magnet for us.

Chapter 5

The Accident

Dear Lynn,

Life here at the ashram is continuing to be intense. I've only been here six days, and I've experienced more spiritually focused exercises, readings, and discourses than I've had over decades in Canada. During the first few days, Swami took us from learning Puja, through a massive multiple wedding ceremony, to fire walking. Through the night, he performed a funeral and cremation for his father, then another double wedding, a birth ceremony for a devotee, and gave a Bahkti Spurana workshop. I've only had six hours of sleep in the last four days. The energy here is subtle but unmistakable.

Our international batch was on our way to Salem yesterday evening (a 5hr drive) in a private bus for hire after we finished attending three days in a row of Shiva discourse in Bangalore. We came across an accident on the highway between a small car and a dump truck, which had left the scene. The car was one of the ashram cars leading our convoy. It was badly smashed, and the occupants were unconscious. A dump truck pulled out to pass and hit the car, rolling it over. The dump truck driver left the scene. Two of us, an American doctor and I, pulled the four injured ashramites out of the wrecked car. There was too much damage to open the doors. We had to rip the smashed windshield out with whatever we could find. A dozen or more onlookers stopped to help, but nobody would touch the broken glass. In a culture of barefoot walkers, broken glass was like Kryptonite.

The people in the car were severely injured and unconscious. We waited quite a while for the ambulance to arrive. I was amazed at how few of the many people who had gathered actually helped. Many people did help themselves to everything in the car: movie cameras, digital SLRs, recording equipment, microphones, and all the cables. Three of Swami's ashramites, including the music director and Swami's brother, were injured. Our organizers found out where the ambulance was taking the accident victims and convinced our bus driver to take us there. By the time we arrived in the small village with a two-room hospital, it was past midnight. Two of the victims were already there. They didn't look good, but all we could do was wait for the doctor on-call to arrive. The American doctor with us was not allowed to touch the victims. It was hard for him to remain a bystander with all his experience. The other two victims arrived shortly after we got there. We did the best we could to help the few people in the hospital to move stretchers and furniture to make room for the four new victims. This place was not equipped to deal with the severity of the four victims' injuries. Arrangements to transfer the victims to the much larger Salem hospital a couple of hours away were quickly organized. Arrangements included using our bus as an ambulance.

Consequently, the event organizers in our group who could speak Tamil or Hindi left in the bus with the victims to the hospital in Salem and to set up for Swami's discourse. There was no room for the rest of us on the bus with four stretchers, so we stayed at the little hospital and waited for the bus to come back for us. All of us non-Tamil speaking internationals were on our own in a small rural Indian town late at night with no means to pay for anything or any way to communicate with anybody. There were too many of us to fit in the tiny waiting room. We stayed together and waited outside in the small dirt parking lot. We were all feeling more than a little vulnerable.

Two policemen chatted and smoked under a nearby fluorescent light strapped to a pole that was the lone street light for as far as we could see. They were standoffish and nervous at the sight of so many international ashram people who couldn't speak Tamil or Hindi. Their curiosity eventually got the better of them. They slowly got closer to check out all of us ashramites in their little village. Their interest in the young teenage girls was making us uncomfortable. I found myself stepping between the policemen and the girls, pretending to be determined to talk to whomever I needed to put the greatest distance between the policemen and our innocent young ashramites. Being six feet six with two five feet six policemen gave me a little confidence to protect our young people, but I was always mindful of appearing to be respectful because they had all the power in the end. We took advantage of the policemen, not understanding English, to share our concerns about the policemen's intentions without being understood by the police. It was a tense few hours until the bus finally returned.

Exhausted, we boarded and quickly settled into the bus. I slept all the way to Salem. The hotel the bus dropped us off at was owned by a Swami devotee, so we all stayed for free. That morning, we found out that Swami was at the hospital before the accident victims arrived. Swami brought them back to consciousness and told them they would be alright, even the one we were told would likely not make it.

We had only slept a couple of hours before being awakened in our hotel room to help set up for the day's discourse and ceremony. All seventeen women, both Indian and Western, stayed in one small Hotel room. The Western women were not happy. We were all quite tired. I had been sick for the past four days and not eating properly, but somehow, Swami's energy keeps you going. Swami stayed in the hotel with us on this first trip to Salem. On the next trip, Swami's car got mobbed, and he was not able to stay with us in the hotel again. Swami told us many Salem devotees invited him to come to Salem, but he didn't have time to respond to all the invitations, so he told them when they could gather five thousand people for a Homa, he would come to Salem. They quickly gathered many times more than five thousand. So here we are.

The empty lot that was being set up for the Homa was just a few blocks down the street from the hotel. As soon as we finished eating, we were sent over to help the organizers set up. Speakers lashed to poles were blaring ear-splitting devotional music at the entrance to the lot. There was no need to ask for directions. I couldn't walk within a block of the speakers without putting my hands over my ears. The audio system sounded like it was set to 100% treble and 0% bass.

We walked between two businesses in the middle of the block to find a surprisingly large grass field behind the stores surrounded by a wall of the backs of the many stores facing the street on all sides. Workers were lashing together eight to twelve-foot bamboo poles over half the field to create a one hundred foot by one hundred foot barn-shaped structure. More volunteers were piling up red bricks at the back to create an elevated platform six feet square for Swami to perform his Homa. There were fifty more small Homa brick structures two feet square arranged in a grid surrounding Swami's platform for devotees to conduct their own Homas with Swami.

We started putting out chairs. I did my best to arrange the chairs in lines with adequate spacing for the next row. By the time the Homa began, there was no evidence of any kind of pattern or arrangement. Indians in this place sit like they drive—comfortably close. The metal roof was peaked with an elevated ridge for ventilation. I asked one of the Indian volunteers why the roof had to be metal to keep out the sun. It was for the rain. Apparently, it always rains when Swami does a big Homa. I was skeptical.

Another volunteer explained that this Homa included a separate puja summoning each of the seven most powerful gods, one for each chakra. As a result, each person in attendance would have all karma and negativity cleared just by being in the presence of such powerful beings. The more powerful the Swami summoning, the more powerful the deities that can be called forth. The offerings burned in the Homa are enticements to attract the deities, and the smoke is believed to be a material the deities can use to take form. We were told to watch the smoke, and we would be able to see the deity's faces if we were sincere. I must not have been sincere enough.

Love,

Karl

I am beginning to notice that a lot of miraculous claims of enlightenment include these little sincerity clauses at the end to shift responsibility for manifestation to the participant. I am still trying to decide if this is a cultural idiosyncrasy or my Western skepticism.

The highway accident experience was terrible. At home, one would think traveling at night was safer, but a lot of commercial traffic moves at night in India when it is cooler. We saw endless lineups of trucks traveling thirty kilometers per hour. Slow enough, you could almost walk faster, but the roads were in such poor repair. Trucks commonly pull out to pass directly into oncoming traffic, and oncoming traffic just moves over to avoid the collision. It is all very respectful and in slow motion. Problems arise where a lane-blocking pothole, big enough to hide a small car, is involved, and both vehicles have to go around the hole. Sometimes, there isn't enough room, and someone is driving through a field or other large holes. The result is a truck bouncing wildly as the driver is thrown off the wooden bench he was sitting on. Wooden benches in trucks are common because they can accommodate more workers.

At that accident scene, I didn't think. I just did what was necessary to help. Later, when there was time, I started to second-guess things I could have done differently. Later for me came when we all had to register with the police because we were at the scene of an accident. I was concerned about how me being part of a police report might affect my travels later. I couldn't refuse. I used the experience to practice detaching myself from possible futures and focused on my happy place inside. From my happy place, I could be more objective about what was happening. There was nothing I could do now, so I would hopefully deal with any fallout when and if any fallout happened.

Thankfully, I was detached enough to notice the potentially illicit intentions of the policemen at the hospital. A guy knows the body language of other guys when they are talking about things they shouldn't. Once again, I felt the need to help despite the risk to myself. My happy place was still there and reassuring me that I was there for a reason. I felt grateful for the opportunity to do my part in concert with the others to protect the group

Chapter 6

The Promise of Brahmacharya Training

Dear Lynn,

Today, I was informed that our phone would get connected tonight. International connectivity will happen the following day. I will call when it is connected. I didn't realize how much I relied on my phone. I finally have regular access to a computer. The ashram bought a new laptop that is mine for the time being. I am typing this message on my bunk instead of in the cramped little library with a lineup of people waiting to do the same. In a couple of days, web editing software will get loaded, and then it is down to work!

I used to feel a welling up of energy when I relaxed into my happy place that I could consciously amplify if I chose to. Now I walk around at fifty percent "happy place" all day long. The energy is focused in my heart center. I don't even have to think about it. It is so freeing to have the comfort of the energy without the effort. I have been jotting down things I would like to share with you when I get a chance. My sense of time is even worse now than it was before. Not having work or bills to pay anymore is a whole new level of holiday.

Swami says he will start a ten-day course from August 13 to 24 to explain the 4 phases of spiritual enlightenment:

1) Brahmacharya: follow the path to enlightenment before reaching puberty.
2) Gersta: following the spiritual path in a traditional life of marriage and work.
3) Marriage agreement: both partners agree to do everything they can to help each other gain enlightenment.
4) Sanyas: concentrated path to enlightenment after a traditional life.

At the end of the course, Swami will choose which phase he will put each of us in. I am just getting bits and pieces of what is involved. I will tell you more as I find out. I tried to call on your birthday. My tech-challenged roommate told me I could use his cell phone, so I made sure it was charged and ready only to find his phone was out of minutes. He is often on his phone, but now I know, only incoming calls. The next morning after Puja, I waited at the office to use their phone. At 9:00 am, I got roped into the next session. The office landline payphone was dead. Apparently, it has been for a week and a half. So here is an epic email instead. Four of us have been waiting two weeks to get our cell phones activated. It's India, and as Swami says, "What can be done?" Apparently, the phone technician has to come to the ashram. Next time I am in Bangalore, I will check out getting a phone and getting it activated at a store.

When we were doing the Nithya Spurana Program (NSP) with Swami, he took us through a healing meditation under the banyan tree. He told us after this exercise that he calls it "the vomiting meditation." He explained that it takes ten thousand imbalanced thoughts to create cancer in a person. This meditation erases all imbalances in your body, and he guarantees that you will never get cancer because you don't have enough life left to create another 10,000 imbalances. Swami says the meditation will not work unless energetically guided by himself. It goes like this:

- Sit on heals with spine straight
- Energetically connect the lower half of your body to the upper half of your body by forming a circle with your thumb and index finger on each hand. Hold these circles against your waist where your upper and lower bodies fold when kneeling. Hold these circles there for the entire meditation.
- Concentrate on your navel
- Visualize white light coming from your navel and exiting your mouth as you chant "uuuuuuu" like the "uu" in vacuum. Not "uuum," just "uuuuuu"
- Chant as long as possible and as loud as possible
- Chant for 10 minutes

- STOP
- Concentrate on your Ananda Ghanda center
- Visualize a white light exiting your heart center, encircling your body, and re-entering your heart center. At the same time
- Bend over and touch the ground with your forehead. Keep circled fingers in place.
- Chant "huuuuuu" like what an owl would sing
- Also, as loudly and as lengthy as possible
- Do this for 10 minutes
- STOP
- Relax for a minute
- Vomit as needed
- Swish oil in your mouth for a minimum of 20 minutes before spitting out.

We did this once each morning for two days. Swami says this method is so simple yet so effective.

The energies at the NSP did not feel as intense but of greater depth and quality. There was always a lot of waiting. I have taken to carrying a book with me everywhere, and I am getting a lot of reading done while I wait. Interestingly, when we returned from a break, the women's side of the meeting hall had an impressive array of blankets, pillows, and other paraphernalia. In contrast, the men's side had virtually nothing.

At Swami's discourse in Bangalore, I got to see how skilled he is in connecting with his audience, starting with a little America bashing. He got lots of applause for praising India's spirituality compared to the West's materialism and how American lawyers are wealthy because Westerners would rather sue than work. He talked about how Western psychologists propagate mental issues by having clients talk about their problems repeatedly to keep them coming back compared to a guru's darshan. He also told the audience that India is the world's spiritual incubator. The West is operating subconsciously, and India is operating consciously. He told the audience that 66% of Americans are depressed compared with 0.06% of Indians. And the Indians that are depressed are the result of cultural invasion from the West. He also said that 80% of Americans die without family around and that 54% are single families in America.

There was thunderous applause to Swami's concession that Indians needed to treat their women better. Swami also said that India's corruption is better than Western corruption because everybody in India is corrupt, so the wealth is distributed more evenly. In the West, only a few at the top benefit. Swami also told a story about being shown the historic route 66 when he was in America. When he told the audience the road was only 160 years old and the whole country wasn't as old as our banyan tree, there was thunderous applause and laughter. Swami told the audience that there is one cop for every 10,000 Indians because 90% of Indians go to some form of worship compared to the West, where less than 2% attend church. The reason for the difference is that there are millions of gods in India, but in the West, there is only one god. He also talked about how the Western media machine is destroying spirituality with TV. Apparently, TV broadcasts at a much higher frame rate than our subconscious can censor. Our subconscious goes into overload, letting in all manner of propaganda to get vomited out onto people at the most inappropriate times. The audience was now rapt and primed for the spiritually enlightening message that followed.

Love,
Karl

The Homa was much the same as the first one to my untrained Western eyes. Now, that I had a better understanding of what a Homa is, I was more aware of what was happening around me. There were a few chai tea vendors with their little one-ounce plastic cups that were so fragile with the hot liquid inside you could only pick them up by the rim. There was a fellow with a big stainless pot filled with water. You could lift the lid and scoop out a cup of water. Indians are very skilled at drinking by pouring the liquid in their mouth without letting the cup touch their lips, so there was only one stainless cup to share with all the people lined up. Nobody seemed to care whether the hand holding the cup while scooping up the water was clean or not.

I gained a new respect for Swami during this Homa. Nobody I talked to saw any faces in the smoke, but his powers of endurance were superhuman. He was up there on his fire pit most of the day, chanting and making offerings. Finally, when the evening ceremonies were completed, Swami gave darshan. The lineup for darshan was endless. Women were on one side and men on the other, but he always had a smile on his face, and all the participants went away happy.

Chapter 7

The Space Within

The next day in the ashram, Swami explained how Shiva described eleven dimensions of reality over ten thousand years ago and how to manipulate them and how *Scientific American* magazine just announced the same thing as a new discovery. To help us understand, Swami held the microphone in front of him, explaining that it has length, width, depth, and space-time, and that as an enlightened being, it would be easy for him to take length and width and put them over here so his hand would appear to pass through the microphone. Of course, many audience members told him to do it. Swami said, "It is too much; you can't take it." He explained that whether we understood what we would see or not, it would be absorbed, and our logic and ego would not be able to deal with it. We were disappointed and said that just being in the master's presence was enough of a miracle.

Swami described our stay at the ashram as being like stones in the Ganges River. We all arrive as stones with our bumps and irregularities, and the master rolls you around in the water, rubbing each stone against the other until you come out polished and smooth. I was surprised at the end of the NSP when two participants came over to me and bowed down on the floor at my feet, as if I was a Swami. But then I realized everybody was doing this to everybody else. They told me it was their way of recognizing and acknowledging the divine in everyone.

This trip to Salem was more relaxed. I was beginning to appreciate a deeper understanding of how things work in India. In my readings and discussions, I discovered a few different methods to take a seeker to enlightenment. Chaos is what Swami uses. It is the hardest on the seeker, but the fastest method. The goal is to break the ego so the mind will become your servant instead of constantly in your face with mindless chatter. Swami says Westerners are the hardest to work on because they have had so much luxury in their lives, but once enlightened, they retain it the best because nothing can tempt them. They have already had a taste of everything!

Chaos forces our issues up to the surface to be acknowledged and ideally absolved. Once absolved, mental space is created. In that space, there is time when confronted with a trigger to step back mentally and to witness what is happening. We can witness the emotion of the trigger rising and hopefully, where or what the trigger is connected to. Just recognizing a trigger is a huge breakthrough because now the normal reaction to that trigger is disconnected, creating an opportunity to discover where that way of reacting came from. In the light of mentally digging for answers, the previously unconscious reaction disappears. This is truly an "ah-ha" moment when the emotional trigger is absolved.

Dear Lynn,

I clearly saw my first aura tonight. I was just staring at the speaker, Rajananda, zoning out, not focusing, and I saw a white halo extending a few inches all around his head. I was able to see the aura at will that whole night. The sight of the aura made me feel like I had achieved a milestone of awareness. However, I haven't been able to do it since, or maybe I should say, I haven't been able to let it happen.

One of the participants in the Bahkti Spurana Program (BSP) was rude to one of the ashramites and was told to leave immediately. He left the program and the ashram as the taxi arrived. It just goes to show you how our unconscious reactions come out at the most inappropriate times.

One morning, we were all sitting around on the front steps of the Ananda Saba when one of the young ashramites nervously asked me which country I was from. He seemed relieved that I was from Canada. He then asked me what my rank was. He was sure I was from the military or police. He was relieved when I told him I was a high school teacher. He smiled and confidently said, "PE teacher!" He had a hard time accepting that I was a computer teacher. But the conversation made relations with all the young ashramites more relaxed. I had no idea they had those kinds of preconceptions.

The last meditation in the BSP was spinning. You stand up straight, extend your arms straight out at shoulder height, and start spinning with your eyes closed. It doesn't take long before you start getting dizzy. Many people fell over onto the concrete floor. When I started feeling dizzy, I stopped and spun in the opposite direction. Reversing the spin direction is hugely disorienting for the first few turns, but it seems to correct the dizziness. I don't know where the idea came from. It just felt like the right thing to do. After reversing direction three or four times, I didn't need to reverse anymore. My body adapted, and I felt like I could spin all day without getting dizzy.

Rajananda had us spin for one hour. Healers got a good workout after our spinning with all the neck issues and bruises from falling over. Spinning was one meditation where my six foot six size was a blessing and a curse. Three young guys wandered wherever their spinning led them, and at various times, they got into my swing area and ended up on the floor. One poor guy got my elbow in his head. I was being careful and peeking a little bit now and then to stay in one spot to avoid hurting other spinners, but the young guys just let loose and spun all over the place.

During the BSP, Rajananda was telling us a story that Swami shared with him. Rajananda complained to Swami about the writing quality in Swami's biography, so Swami made Rajananda his biographer. One of the stories Rajananda was to include in Swami's memoir about his early ashram days was when he and his friends would open the newspaper and select an article at random and travel to that location. This particular time the article chosen was about a temple that is rarely accessible because of being submerged by the water level of the lake there. Swami initially said no because the location was too far away, but as soon as he saw the picture of the temple, his face changed as if he were no longer in control of his body, and off they went.

The trip was long, and Swami didn't say a word. When they got to the lake, Swami got out of the car and walked so fast along the lake toward the temple that nobody could keep up. One by one, they had to stop to rest, but one of Swami's friends was very concerned about Swami's state of mind and jogged along to make sure he was alright.

When Swami got to the foot of the temple stairs, he stared up at the top of the stairs in awe. Then he looked over at his friend and asked, "Do you see?" The friend listed off the ruined temple parts that he could see: the pillars, the steps, the carvings, and so on. Swami looked disappointed and asked, "You can't see?" Swami led his young friend up the stairs to touch one of the pillars. As soon as the young friend touched the pillar, he was almost overcome by an intense wave of blissful energy. When he regained his senses, he saw a man sitting on the throne in front of him at the top of the steps in his mid-fifties. It was a different body, but there was no doubt that it was Swami. Then he became aware of the whole scene. He recognized many of the ashramites, but they were in different bodies.

It was hundreds of years ago, and he was witnessing the preparations for the energizing ceremony that was about to take place.

Swami was an enlightened master at that time in history. He was part of a large group of enlightened masters assembled to ground the universal energy to help maintain balance in the earth at that time and into an uncertain future. The masters had already performed the grounding ceremony successfully for the water element in the Ganges. Now they intended to ground earth energy into a giant lingam meticulously prepared over many years in the temple. Swami, in this past incarnation, had carefully groomed many yogis to help him perform this grounding. He traveled the length and breadth of India to gather the best 18 yogis to handle the tremendous amount of energy that needed to be grounded. Now the ceremonies, calculations, and preparations were finished, it was time to do the work and ground the energy. All was ready for the grounding. Swami and the 18 yogis took their positions around the huge lingam inside the temple.

Swami started to bring the Universal energy down. The incredible power was too much for two of the yogis, and they fell into fear of being harmed. As soon as the energy of fear appeared, the whole energy field changed from love to fear. Swami would not ground fear energy into the lingam, so he immediately dissipated the energy. The energy dissipation created a massive shock wave, and Swami says he has no memory of what happened after that. He knows he will complete his mission to ground the energy into a lingam in the present time. Swami told Rajananda that two people currently at his ashram don't know they are reincarnations of the original yogis, and Swami is looking for the remaining sixteen. This story has the ashramites always checking out new arrivals to see if they might be one of Swami's missing yogis.

A month ago, an interesting corroboration came when a swami from another ashram a few hours away came and donated his ashram to Swami. That swami told Rajananda in a private conversation about the temple story to consider that our swami selected the site for this ashram from a vision he had of the banyan tree here. Furthermore, he was to consider that our banyan tree was distinctive and well established in that period, and the old lingam temple was easily within walking distance for a yogi who might have become despondent at that time. The Swami made it all too clear that the swami's bones found under the banyan tree in the small one meter stone temple were likely our swami's from that previous incarnation, and that is why there is such a strong connection to this place for Swami. Also, Swami's vision of the new temple currently under construction would house a huge lingam, and that might be why Swami's pool has a huge lingam in it. After hearing these stories, another ashramite and I looked at each other with goosebumps and decided we must each be one of the missing sixteen yogis.

Love,

Karl

Swami's story illustrates how intricately interwoven our lives are for reasons we may never understand in this life. Similarly, events for me fell into place when I was working in construction, looking for a better career. As a construction worker, I worked for a company that had me installing equipment in a senior care facility.

Working in the facility for a few months, I got to talk with some of the residents. They helped me understand what my life could be like in the future, sitting in this place in my own wheelchair, wondering what life could have been like if I had followed my heart and become a teacher. I decided to leave my career in construction and become a teacher. Once decided, everything mysteriously/synchronistically fell into place.

Shortly after that job, I worked on another construction job installing equipment in a school, which provided me with an opportunity to talk to a teacher who was doing the job I pictured myself doing. I got to find out enough about teaching to get excited. The teacher also knew the teacher program recruiter and set up an interview for me. At the end of the interview,

I was conditionally accepted into the teaching program. Two years later, I sold my house and moved to the coast with my young family to attend university. After three years of university, I accepted my first teaching assignment.

The whole journey to become a teacher was an enchanting exercise in synchronicity. There were many challenges that pushed me far outside my comfort zone in ways I couldn't have imagined, but then synchronicity would bring me just what I needed. My qualifications in construction were always there to support my family and me during summers and in the time between my first few teaching jobs. I will always be thankful for the wisdom to recognize enough of life's little nudges before life had to use a two by four.

Dear Lynn,

Today, I was invited to a meeting with Swami, Danika, Pierre, and Priya to discuss our work on the ashram website. We met in front of one of the grass huts. During our meeting, someone drove their shiny new little car through the no-public-entry gate up into the ashram. Someone should have stopped the vehicle at the gatehouse, even if the driver was known. I have only seen delivery vehicles allowed past the gatehouse, and this car was driving too fast for the narrow walking paths between the gardens. The vehicle was not a delivery tuk-tuk. It looked like a small brand-new vehicle. We all watched with astonishment as the vehicle turned onto the path we were standing on. I held my breath as the car stopped way too close to our group.

Swami didn't seem to be concerned in the least, as if it were no different than a person walking up to him. One of our group reminded me that Indian people have no personal space. The driver, an ashramite, jumped excitedly out of her new car and asked Swami to bless her new car. I was shocked that anybody could be so casual about such a request of Swami. These types of requests were becoming Swami's new normal. While Swami took care of the blessing, our webmaster found her laptop and got it plugged in to show Swami our website progress.

Swami's evaluation of the website took 5 minutes. The meeting went on for an hour more discussing what Swami wanted to see on the site and how it should be worded and linked. In the end, Swami glared at Priya and told her, "All these things I told you six months ago. This meeting is over. Go and get it done." After the meeting, Swami slowly walked away with a blissful smile on his face. Oh, to be so detached. The three of us hurried to the library, where the only internet connection was, so I could show them some other things I had created for the website.

One of our group was a graphic designer who would make pictures, backgrounds, and animations for the website; the other fellow was a computer programmer. Priya was a businesswoman from a wealthy family with no web experience. Swami's methods involve pushing people out of their comfort zone, so two years ago, he had told her she was the ashram's new webmaster. Our webmaster has been teaching herself ever since.

Swami decided we should abandon the current website and create six new interlinked sites. I was looking forward to the challenge, but cautious about how life at this ashram could change plans in a heartbeat.

A long-time devotee conducted the healer's initiation at the ashram. He was a corporate trainer and a good speaker. He told us that the Western one-day healer's initiation was called Tantra Initiation in India and was only good enough to heal yourself. To be a truly powerful healer, we needed to do the two-day Yoga Initiation that was done in India, and we were to follow all the healer's living conditions, including adopting a vegan diet and minimizing your impact on the environment. When Swami arrived at the end of the Yoga Initiation to give us the healer's initiation, he told us that the healing is just a by-product. Enlightenment is what is being given.

When I received my darshan from Swami, the intensity of the energy blew my little fist-sized Ananda Ghanda center wide open so that it felt like my whole chest was lit up and throbbing, radiating bliss. The energy felt deeper and more potent than anything I have ever felt before. I was blissed-out like I have never been blissed-out before.

Love,
Karl

Swami pushes us outside our comfort zones to show us how our minds create artificial limitations. Limitations unwittingly taught by our parents and other significant people we held in high regard when we were young. Limitations accepted by a naive receptive mind. We are capable of so much more than our limited minds can imagine. The goal here is to dissolve our mind's self-imposed limits. That's how seeming magic happens, by getting our mind and it's perceived limitations out of the way.

In this new limitless state, we don't know the impossible. We have created the space for peace of mind to hear our intuition and to be open to a whole new world of possibilities. Swami pushes us to see what it is to stand outside our comfort zone and look back in to force our minds to expand.

I had wanted access to the internet on the ashram, but there was only one computer hooked up to the one dial-up connection. The queue for the use of this single computer was long, with ashram business always taking precedence. Now I had the access I wanted in the form of my new website laptop. I didn't need to compose emails at the one connected computer. I could compose my emails at my convenience on the laptop and send them late at night when the connection didn't drop as often while uploading website updates. Synchronicity provides everything we ask for, subject to conditions such as doing no harm and advancing our life plan.

Chapter 8
Chaotic Temple Tours

Dear Lynn,

Our Tiruvannamalai trip started when Swami held a meeting with all us English-speaking international devotees. We have been here for about a month now and have been growing impatient with our desires to do more and feel like we are being taken more seriously. Up to this point, we have had few lessons and rarely in English. Appointments for training have often left us wondering where our trainer is. We feel like we are unwelcome and an inconvenience.

We were all asked to submit our questions and concerns to one incredibly overworked Priya responsible for us. Swami gave her fire (scolding). He told her that all these questions should be her job to answer. We were incredibly disappointed that Swami didn't address any of our questions. His response was to give us more time to get all our questions answered and to adjust to living on the ashram.

Swami told us he would start a ten-day brahmacharya training program, at the end of which he would decide who would become a brahmachari. One of our group asked what the qualifications were for brahmacharya training. Swami laughed and said, "You are breathing! That's all the qualification you need." After returning from his trip to America, he will start an intensive training program of six classes per day! Swami then told us that he had to go and put a fire under the deity makers and that we should all go together for an adventure. An adventure it was!

Our temple adventure started on August 11. We assembled by the eating huts with our bags packed for two nights away. We were all ready by 10:00 am, as requested. The convoy of small cars finally left at about 4:00 pm. It was one more case of hurry-up-and-wait for a five-hour trip to Salem. The car I started in was tiny. I went to get into the front seat, and unbelievably, the driver told me to get into the back. It wasn't as bad as I thought it was going to be, but still very tight for a 6'6" guy. When the trip organizer saw me sitting in the back of the car, he laughed, gave the driver a firing, and told me to get in the front seat. The front seat was better but still tight. We took the same road that the ashramites had the accident on a few weeks previously. This time Swami was in the lead car of our four-car convoy.

An hour into our trip, while driving through Bangalore, our little car got a flat. The driver pulled over, muttering something about never having ever changed a flat tire before and did anybody know how to do it. When we got out of the car, we were amazed to discover we were stopped at the curb directly in front of a tire repair shop. The shop replaced the tube, and we were on our way in no time. Talk about synchronicity! Synchronicity, the seeming random confluence of events that, in hindsight, appear to be orchestrated by a higher power. The driver told us that he did not bring any cash and asked if we ashramites in the car could chip in and pay for the work. Everybody looked at everybody else. Ashramites don't carry money.

I paid the 250.00rs ($6CAD) bill and was graciously rewarded with the nail pulled from the tire as a receipt. Quite a while later, the driver pulled into a petrol station and put 500.00rs into the tank and once again asked us to share the cost of the fuel. I paid for the bill again. This driver showed us the ultimate in trusting the Universe to find the money, or else he was an excellent con artist. I'm pretty sure he was the latter. This driver was a trusted friend of some of the ashramites. I'd spent 750.00rs, and we hadn't even stopped for food yet. We arrived at the hotel in Salem at about midnight. We never did stop for food.

The trip takes longer at night with all the slow-moving lorries on the road. Picture a truck made in 1940 that struggles with an undersized engine and slows to a crawl on hills. There are endless lines of these trucks. As soon as traffic breaks, they all pull into the oncoming lane together to try and pass the one or two lorries going 1 or 2 km slower than they are. Some of these lorries that are passing are also being passed. It now looks more like a slow-motion freeway than a divided highway. The humor comes when another truck approaches in the oncoming lane. All the trucks jockey for an opening back into their original lane. Now add to this impossible comedy a road with potholes deep enough to hide a small car in. The lorries are swerving all over the place, driving down the shoulders to avoid potholes or just plain stopping if the hole is too deep or too big to avoid. Then they drive through the hole at a crawl. The smart ones are the ones still in their lane being passed. Whenever a village is located by the road, there are either speed bumps or traffic gates 200 feet apart that force traffic to slow to zig-zag around them.

The next morning in the hotel, we got a 4:00 am wake up call to be ready to leave at 5:00 am. When I got downstairs, I was asked to change seats with one of the ashramites in the women's car. I happily agreed to give up my squishy front seat in the little car for the front seat in a much larger Sumo Bata, which looks like an Indian version of a Land Rover. The leg room was only slightly better than in the little car, but the headroom was great. I found out from the girls who traveled in the Sumo Bata that there was some drama in the car. They were happy to have one less girl in the car. Everybody was happy.

Besides the two front seats in this Sumo Bata, there was a three-person bench seat behind the front seats that had four people on it, and behind that, two small single seats were facing each other in the very back that four people managed to squeeze into. That's ten people in a vehicle designed for a maximum of seven.

Then Swami's driver came over to our vehicle with an adult male who needed to go halfway with us and be dropped off a couple of hours down the road. We tried our best to say no, but Swami's driver told us we had to work it out as the other cars left. Fortunately, one of our passengers was a slight, young pre-teen.

Petra moved into the front seat with me. The new guy squished into the mini-bench in the very back. I got claustrophobic just seeing the poor guy all squished into that little seat. Our vehicle was so overloaded we couldn't even get out of the driveway from the hotel. It was hanging so low with all the people in it. We all had to get out to move down the ramp and onto the level ground in the alley. We all squeezed back in, and away we went.

The vehicle rode like a boat. There is no weight limit for vehicles in India, only capacity, including city buses. As long as there is room, it is all good. I have seen ticket takers in buses taking fares from each person hanging on the outside of a city bus. We caught up with the slow-moving convoy before too long. Just another example of how Swami works on you without you knowing it!

We dropped off our rider as planned. It felt like a lot longer trying to sit on half a bucket seat with a chatty little 12-year-old. Fortunately, she slept more than she talked, being unaccustomed to getting up at 4:00 am, but then I had to hold onto her to keep her in the seat because the road was often very bumpy, and the driver was making wild swerving motions unexpectedly to avoid the biggest potholes or to avoid the cars driving head-on in our lane as they tried to pass someone in their lane. Near Kumbakonam, two men waved the convoy into a driveway. Later, we discovered the driveway belonged to a fellow whom Swami befriended on his spiritual wanderings. Swami sent us all on ahead as he enjoyed lunch with his friend.

In the village of Kumbakonam, we had lunch at a restaurant. It was much better than the ashram food. The restaurant washrooms were through the disheveled kitchen out the back, down six or eight black, greasy, cluttered stairs, down a narrow sidewalk that reeked of urine with six crude-looking corrugated metal doors that provided a modicum of privacy for the traditional hole-in-the-floor toilets. Guys and girls all took turns using the same stalls. Most of the girls refused to use them partly due to the rough-looking men hanging out smoking around the dark, uninviting toilets, watching us and talking loudly. Even with years of construction-site, temporary-toilet experience, this was disgusting.

From the restaurant, we went to the first temple. We learned that our guide was the top temple designer in India (Swami's words). Unfortunately, the designer's explanations were all in Tamil. We English speakers got translations, but there seemed to be more Hindi spoken than the English translation. We were told that this temple covered 67 acres and was the tallest temple in the world at over 270'.

There were about 11 of us international devotees, called the Outside Inmates by the Indian ashramites, plus four brahmacharis and a few dignitaries. We got the royal tour. The designer took us to all the places the public aren't allowed to go and waved us through all the temple lineups to view the different Pujas that were on hold till we got there and could see each one start to finish. We ran with our soft Western feet on smoking hot Indian cobblestoned plazas between each Puja to quickly get to the next one. One of the brahmacharis who was born and raised in Bangalore told us it would take a month to coordinate the timing of all the pujas to be able to see what we just viewed in a few hours. An impressive display of coordination in any culture, but monumental in this one.

The synchronicity of all of us being able to follow our tour guide and not lose anybody in the crush of bodies we forced our way through to get to the front of lines held in queue by a maze of steel gates was incredible. On the way out of the enormous temple, an elephant turned the end of its trunk up for you to drop coins into. The elephant would then drop the coins into its Mahout's hands before blessing you by plopping the end of its trunk on your head. Unsanitary on so many levels, but auspicious to be blessed by an elephant while escorted by a swami.

We all got back into our convoy of vehicles where we had left them outside the front gates, where only staff were allowed to park. All our feet were sore and hot. All temples are sacred ground, so shoes you want to wear again are left in the car.

Swami's car led our convoy to the next town, which was much smaller than our first stop. The vehicles were squeezing their way down narrow market streets. I was contemplating rolling up the window despite the heat because everything and everybody was so close, but then Swami's vehicle stopped, and he jumped out. We were off again without warning. We quickly dropped our sandals in our car and ran after Swami. He was working on us still.

This temple was a very famous healing temple. Once again, the lineups of people in the temple snaked out of sight down dark stone corridors. Still, our guide breezed past them all with a few words to the many guards who were everywhere, and special gates were opened for us so we could bypass all the lineups and get to see the beautiful brass deities in no time. Even with the exclusive access, it took a lot of walking and running to see all the deities and their respective pujas. With some of the deities, we had to mix with the public to get close enough to see. One of the monks made a couple of wisecracks about having to get a ladder if he had to place the blessing bowl on my head.

Synchronistically, at this point in writing this email to send to you, Lynn, Swami came into the library and talked to those of us waiting for our turn at the internet computer about the temple trip. After asking me if I enjoyed the trip and me nodding affirmatively, he said that it had to be spontaneous and fast like that, or there would be so many people lining the roads to pay their respects to him that the car would never be able to move. He said that the few dignitaries who organized the trip at the last minute leaked the information, and the next morning, when leaving the place he stayed in Salem, many people were lining the road at 6:00 am.

To continue, after the last Puja, we rushed out of the temple to our vehicles, still waiting in the crowded street. Being a Swami, you get the best parking spots! Swami jumped into his vehicle at the front door, and we were left to search for our vehicle and then run to get in so the driver didn't lose sight of Swami's vehicle and could follow because, as far as we knew, there was no plan. Now we know Swami and the Designer were the only ones who knew the program.

We followed Swami's car through a maze of back streets and saw more of the typical Indian life. Villages are much cleaner off the beaten path. People take pride in their homes. We noticed some people sweeping the street in front of their houses. We also saw people sleeping on mats and cots outside on the dirt at their front doors. Our convoy ended up in the country, traveling down a small dusty country lane at a deity manufacturer's business.

The business site was mostly an open dirt yard in the middle of tall trees and grass fields with a few ancient shacks. I was pleasantly surprised to discover that they were making the deities the same way I have my high school students in my metalwork class build projects. The deity makers start with a crude sculpture of welded concrete, reinforcing rods and heavy wire. The rods and wire are then packed carefully with soft wax to skillfully sculpt the statue's final shape.

Once the final shape is approved, the sculpture gets covered in thin layers of mud. The mud is allowed to dry thoroughly between coats. The whole sculpture is then gently placed in a sandpit deep enough to cover the entire sculpture with sand. Sticks are positioned as the sculpture is buried to act as channels to pour in the molten bronze. Then the bronze is heated up, zinc and copper, the color of fire! The molten bronze is poured strategically into selected stick holes (sprues and runners) so the vaporized wax can escape from the other holes. The bronze is hot enough if poured at the right speed that it vaporizes all the wax as it fills every little space that was wax.

Days later, after the sculpture cools enough, the workers dig it out, and the long process of cleaning and polishing starts. They use hammers and chisels to knock off the hardened mud and hand files to take off the remaining scale. This process hasn't changed in centuries.

The deity currently under construction was destined for Swami's Los Angeles center. It was about 50% cleaned up. Swami wasn't translating any of this process to us, so I explained the process to a few interested people. In the middle of my "lesson," Swami came over and listened for a minute, confirming my explanation of runners, sprues, and pouring the molten bronze into the buried wax sculpture before he moved into one of the sheds to look at other deities. Swami spent a lot of time fussing about the exact expression and details of his life-sized deity currently in its sculpted wax form. I discovered from one of the dignitaries that the deity still in its wax form is intended to be Swami's likeness with a female on his lap. The pose of which is to emulate Ananda Eashwari.

Swami wanted the chin to change a little. We quietly felt the sculptor had crafted a very realistic likeness of Swami, including his chin. Even at Swami's enlightenment level, there was still enough ego to be concerned about how his chin appeared. Swami's concern gave us all a glimpse into what enlightenment might be like. We all piled back into our cars and waited while Swami spent an hour in the office negotiating a delivery date of September 1, 2006.

Then it was off again! The temple adventure continued. The next temple was huge, filled with a maze of hallways and staircases. I was lost soon after entering. If I didn't have the group to follow from Puja to Puja, I could have spent days trying to find my way out. After each Puja, the priests gave us something to put on our foreheads. I had white ash on my forehead, orange powder on my third eye, the traditional red dot (bindi) to inspire all who see it, a streak of yellow powder up the middle of my forehead, and sprinklings of sacred water from the rest. One of this temple's big claims to fame was that the mummy of the founding Swami is in a special room in the temple. As special guests of the designer and escorts of Swami, we got to see the mummy.

The mummified Swami was wrapped in the sitting position with his hand held up with the palm facing the viewer as if giving darshan. The mummified Swami is said to have arranged his body so that when he left his body, it would stay in that pose. Apparently, it has been in that pose for a thousand years. In another deity room, there was a diminutive deity who was allegedly Shiva. When I commented on the small size in such a vast temple, Shiva's massive reclining statue laying behind the deity was pointed out. The head was 4' in diameter and the remainder was behind a long curtain.

The temple designer led us up to the roof onto a small viewing platform to see all the temples in the town shortly before dark. The temple we were on was in the middle of a north-south line of 14 temples. There were just as many temples at right angles to the first 14. Ironically, we were at the center of a cross of temples. This designer knew how to navigate all the temples and how they were all built. My translator could not keep up. The hot paving stones were thankfully a little cooler in the evening shadows. We were still running in our soft Western bare feet to keep up with Swami. Despite Swami's bright orange robes, we still lost him from time to time. We just had to look for a large mob of people. Temple visitors would flock around

Swami for blessings as he passed. He seemed to breeze through them effortlessly. We, on the other hand, did not have Swami's navigation powers to move through the crush of blessing seekers to keep up.

Back in the vehicles again! We didn't travel very far this time. A big street party stopped us. There was a band playing, and flower leis being handed out. Everybody wore their finest with flower petals strewn all over the street. It was a welcome back party at the temple designer's house for all of us. His home was just as humble as any other on the street. You would never know by looking at his house that he had designed the largest, most sacred buildings in India.

Inside, Swami was directed to sit on the only chair in the house—the only chair not carefully piled up behind the house, that is. People paraded through the house in an endless line for energy darshan and healing. I was sure they were all running around the house and coming in the front door again for a second darshan. We all sat on a big mat on the floor around Swami and watched.

Pictures were taken. Finally, we were ushered into the next room for the evening meal at around nine o'clock. Like the first room, all the furniture had been removed, so there was enough room for everybody to sit on the beautiful marble floor. A stainless plate with a fresh palm leaf was placed in front of each of us. Servers put rice and sauces and sweets on our plates. The food was amazing. As people were getting full, one of the brahmacharis came in and told us to finish up because Swami wanted to leave. We gratefully held our hands as if in prayer, bowed gratitude to our hosts, and were whisked off to a devotee's hotel in Salem.

We arrived at the hotel at 1:30 am. Three of us guys comfortably shared a beautiful large room. I don't even remember washing up. The seven girls somehow shared a small room with two double beds. At 4:30 am, we got a wake-up call to be ready to leave at 5:00 am. We hadn't even unpacked our bags from the night before, so gathering up our few belongings was quick, but waking up was a longer process. There was a lot of eye rubbing as we stood at the curb holding each other up. Five in the morning was an excellent time to close my eyes and get a little meditation.

Swami didn't arrive, which was not entirely out of character for someone of his popularity. We waited and waited until 10:30 am when a call came through. Swami had stayed at one of the ashramite's private home last night. When Swami got in his car in the morning, there were so many worshipers, the car could barely move. At one point, the worshipers rocked the car and scared everybody.

Swami directed the driver to drive straight to the ashram. Our driver had no such problems with us and easily stopped for coffee and lunch. A few of us asked the driver if we could stop at the pizza place on Brigade Road in Bangalore. He said, "Yes," so the rest of us waited for lunch in Bangalore. The driver kept saying "yes" whenever we reminded him. He just kept saying yes and kept on driving. He never did stop. I suspect "yes" was the only English word he knew.

Love,

Karl

After our amazing temple tours, we international "Outside Inmates" felt a lot better about being acknowledged as participants in ashram affairs. We were still treated as outsiders by some of the ashramites, which was perfectly understandable. We hadn't been raised in a beautiful, indigenous, ascension culture. We had very little understanding of the depth of devotion and meaning of many ceremonies going on in the ashram. Living on an Ashram with a guru was far more sacred than anything we Westerners could appreciate. We were being offered an intimate glimpse into the heart of culture with thousands of years of history and evolution. There was so much to understand and appreciate, but the depth and profundity of what an ashram had to offer could only be truly experienced from an indigenous Indian's perspective. For example, I was surprised to discover that Swami had adopted two young ashramites at their parent's request. No matter how hard I try to adopt an Eastern perspective, I could never give over one of my sons to anybody. This just demonstrates how shallow my Western understanding of Swami devotion is. I pray for more understanding.

Chapter 9

10 Days of Brahmacharya Training

Dear Lynn,

It is day 1 of brahmacharya training. After our usual morning of Guru Puja under the banyan tree, all prospective brahmacharis met in the Ananda Saba meeting hall. When Swami arrived, he told us to meditate on our Ananda Ghanda center in the middle of our chests, to keep our eyes closed, and not to open them at any cost. We would get further instructions when it was time. Thoughts of waiting for hours for buses and meetings that sometimes never manifested taunted us. Sitting and meditating with eyes closed, forgotten for days, was a real possibility in this ashram. Our egos at work again, we meditated for about an hour until Swami recited a Sanskrit prayer to end the meditation and to start the training.

Swami told us that it was his job to make sure we were all successful. Then he blessed us in a big booming voice, saying, "You will all be successful," in a very powerful, raise-the-hair-on-the-back-of-your-neck way three times. He continued to tell us how tricky the ego can be, but now was the time to surrender, not intellectually, but from the being level. I had no idea what that meant or how I could accomplish such a feat.

Swami put us into meditation again for another hour or so. The meditation on our Ananda Gandha center before the blessing was calm and peaceful, like the workshop meditations. After the Be Successful Blessing, the energy welling up inside me was intense. The blessing was working. My question was answered, and I was experiencing the being level. Of course, the blessing had worked.

I sat in boundless bliss, floating gently inside my body. Visions of past emotional traumas played out in my mind's eye without attachment, but with a strong pull to surrender all that I saw. Each childhood event I witnessed and surrendered was like unplugging another appliance from my mental house wall. As each appliance was unplugged, the lights got brighter, everything worked more naturally, and small waves of energy washed over me. After a few "appliances" were unplugged, the tears started rolling down my face. They didn't stop for the whole meditation. I was euphoric.

Swami finished with an energy darshan, but this time he pulled us in gently for a hug and held each one of us with his thumb on our third eye for a good minute. It was the most intense energy darshan I have ever had. The rest of the day, I felt like I was walking 6" off the ground, and the bliss didn't abate until I drifted off to sleep that night.

Day 2 of brahmacharya training. Swami spent a lot of time explaining and making sure that each of us understood all five brahmacharya conditions and the seriousness of the commitment required.

1. No meat or eggs
2. No sex or relationships
3. No drugs or alcohol
4. No property
5. 100% commitment to master and his mission

Number two and four are so there is nobody and nothing to run away from the guru to. One student told Swami he owned an apartment. Swami said, "It is mine, sign it over, and it is done!" Swami said, "You think I'm fooling! I'm not!" We Westerners still didn't understand we were committing to anything more serious than going to a university to earn a degree. Swami told us we should be prepared to fast for three days to help cleanse. We should also be ready to beg for our food away from the ashram for three days, and the best part is that we would be meditating in a fire for 8 hours to burn our ego and mental bodies so that we could be reborn without subconscious conditioning.

After lunch, we were directed by Swami's assistant Rajananda to meditate once again on our Ananda Gandha center. After about an hour, Swami took more time to explain how we were making a significant choice that could not be stopped once started. Brahmacharya training is a surgery of the spirit. You cannot get up off the operating table halfway through a medical surgery; in the same way, you cannot leave the brahmacharya training halfway through without incurring severe spiritual consequences.

Swami explained that part of the brahmacharya training process involves him shutting down all our chakras to experience death without losing the physical body. He will then restart us, but we will not be connected with the mind or ego the same way. We will experience life more like a witness to our lives and be unaffected by them. Sexual desire will be gone. Our energies will be much higher. This rise in frequency and intensity will give us tremendous power, but without a connection to our ego's guidance, we will be able to lower our vibration as easily as lift it. We can become demons or devils just as easily as enlightened. This is why it is so important that we don't leave the spiritual surgery table until Swami finishes the re-programming of us. If we cannot vow to complete the training, he will not allow us to start. Swami made it clear that he is not responsible for us if we leave the training before it is completed.

The gravity and depth of the commitment were starting to sink in. I learned more by talking with other ashramites about how sacred Indians perceive the opportunity to be trained as a brahmachari by a swami. A brahmachari in the family is a huge blessing for the whole family. The blessing will affect all branches on the family tree for generations to come. That is one reason a family may ask a swami to adopt one of their children.

Day 3 of brahmachari training. Again we were directed by Rajananda to meditate on our Ananda Gandha centers after our regular three hours of morning puja, prayers, and meditation under the banyan tree. We ended up meditating about 4 hours this time. After our meeting, we re-assembled in the meeting hall after lunch. We waited and waited and waited.

Swami finally came in about six pm. He took one look at our mystified faces, and with his typically enigmatic smile, he told us that he wanted to make sure we all had time to run away if we could not meet all the conditions.

Swami described how fantasy shuts down the root chakra and how ancient meditation techniques were not designed to deal with broadcast media depicting actors pretending to act out fantasies. Media created a double layer of fantasy that didn't exist when these techniques were brought into the world by the old masters. The next meditation we did was designed to force our root chakra open. The meditation starts by covering your senses, using the left hand on the left side of the face and the right hand on the right side of the face. I covered my eyes with my pointer fingers, plugged my nostrils with my second fingers, plugged my ears with my thumbs, and used my remaining fingers to cover my mouth. The result is not hearing, seeing, smelling, tasting, or breathing all at the same time. Once our hands are in place, we hold our breath and chant the word "Lam" in our mind until we feel light-headed and nearly pass out. When we do this meditation correctly, we will feel a burst of energy in our root chakra in the last second before releasing our hands, similar to a sexual orgasm, as our root chakra opens. Swami told us that once is enough if you feel the orgasm. I felt the energy burst on my second attempt. We repeated the process five times and then five more times the next day to make sure everybody experienced the opening.

We broke for the evening meal and returned to the meeting hall, where we waited and waited. Close to midnight, we were called back to the food temples to wait some more.

Young ashramites came in and set up the sound system for Swami to address us as we were handed a brahmacharya release form to sign. We were a little intimidated by some of the points. There was the usual willing participant, physically fit, and volunteer to work to spread Swami's vision as he sees fit. Still, the parts about tantric methods of male and female ecstasy and sexual energy, along with images of graphic depictions, were a little concerning. We all signed the release despite our concerns. After all, this was a very conservative ashram where meetings and dances were gender-segregated with women and men on opposite sides of the hall.

After a bit of discussion about the release with Swami, we moved back to the Ananda Saba and watched videos about masters of the past. Unpredictably, Swami would get up and walk around in the audience, and anybody he found sleeping would get a crack on the head with his cane. I didn't remember anything about a cane on the release form. I expected these videos to be informative; they felt more like a stay-awake challenge. I was up to the challenge.

Day 4 of brahmacharya training. Today is Krishna's birthday, a national holiday for India. He is about 5600 years old. I haven't seen that birthday on Google yet. It is also India's independence day, but independence takes a distant back seat to Krishna. Every ashram in India has some celebratory ceremony today, so Swami held a small puja for Krishna and recited some Sanskrit verses for us with a short discourse on Krishna's contribution to India. Everyone got spoons full of sweet rice and a couple of Indian sweets. A few of us got our mouths stuffed full of sweets with a big Swami laugh. We had to eat them as Swami shoved them in. "It's tradition!" Everybody at the ashram came in for the sweet giving. There was lots of dancing while everybody got their turn to have Swami stuff their faces with sweets.

Brahmacharya training that evening started with an admonishment that nobody held their breathe longer than 60 seconds. We did the root chakra (suffocation) meditation five more times. After lunch, we went up to the parade square near the banyan tree and laid out circles to set on fire for our meditation. We had no idea how the circles would be set on fire. We had visions of sitting atop a pile of firewood while someone set the pile on fire. What Swami actually did was have us lay on the ground with arms stretched up over our heads, and someone marked the ground at our toes and fingertips. We then used strings to make the two marks into the circumference of a large circle.

I was offered money to lay down for other people's marks, as I am six foot six and make a pretty big circle. When we returned to the Ananda Saba, Swami had us run on the spot with our eyes closed till we dropped. No moving when we can't run anymore, just drop. I peeked a few times and was surprised to see the younger boys lying on the ground while I was still running. They were smarter than I was just to give it their all and then relax. I tried to pace myself and ended up running way too long. When I finally gave up, there weren't many left. Swami then got us to pull out the extra mattresses stacked in the meeting hall storage room. They were all kinds of dirty, but it was better than laying on a concrete floor. Some boys found cots, and we all slept in the Ananda Saba together. Swami told us that when he leaves his body during the night, the hall will fill with his consciousness, our bodies will become his, and we will experience what it is like to be in his body. I couldn't sleep all night.

Swami told us later that all these rituals are not necessary to reach enlightenment. We can become enlightened instantly with a simple touch with enough intensity. Unfortunately, the enlightenment will not stick until we have done the work to get there ourselves. The rituals are being done so they can be recorded for whoever needs a record in the future.

Day 5 of brahmacharya training. This morning, Swami got us up an hour later at about 6:30. We were all energized and ready to greet the day. I had virtually no inner mind chatter and an amazing well of energy in my chest. Others had similar experiences. He asked if anybody had a dreamless sleep. About one-third of the group put their hands up. Swami said, “Good!” after 1-2-3 (bathroom break), Swami told us that last night he cleared all the karma that we had brought into this life and all that we had collected during this life. Now he was going to empty the well of karma that we had accumulated over countless lifetimes. We dip into this well of karma when we build our next incarnation. Swami told us to prepare for this meditation by feeling completely open, such that a gentle breeze would flow right through us unimpeded so that he could get in and do his work.

We waited and waited until 3:30 when we went up to the parade ground to place wood and dried cow patties around our fire circles. We sat down in our circles at 4:00 pm to meditate and stifled our chuckles as all attempts to light the sticks and cow patties failed. It was more like smoked brahmacharya than meditating in a ring of fire. We went back to the Ananda Saba and exorcised our karma that we had accumulated during incarnations as animals. We acted, as completely as possible, like the animal that felt right for us. We slept in the Ananda Saba again. We were not allowed to take time to wash or brush teeth, just grab a blanket, lie down, and sleep.

Chapter 10

A Mile in Swami's Shoes

Day 6 of brahmacharya training, Begging Day. Girls were sent out in two large groups to a local village south of the Ashram and were not allowed to go to the main road. Boys were told to go to the nearest town, Bidadi, and beg, wander around for a while, and then come back and present their alms to the master. We were not to bother anybody by knocking on doors or disrupting business. As Swami was leaving the Ananda Saba, I quietly asked him if I could wear my sandals on my soft Western feet. He laughed and said nobody would give if I wore sandals.

On the way out of the Ananda Saba, I made a quick stop in my room to lighten my load, leave my water bottle, and such. When I came out, the girls were already gone, and the boys were a quarter mile down the road. My tender bare Western feet moved as fast as they could down the gravel road. I wasn't catching up very quickly. Fortunately, an Indian ashramite was returning on his motorcycle with some shopping. All the boys ahead of me had to stop and see. I caught up to the group just as they started walking again. It took all my concentration and will power to keep up with them once they started moving again. We took a side road to Bidadi through a very small village and started our begging with the first people we met. I felt guilty asking the poor villagers for anything, seeing what their living conditions were like. Still, Swami assured us that it is part of Indian culture to give to your community, and everybody knows about the ashram. It is an honor to give to someone on a spiritual quest. West and East diverge on this topic more than any other, in my opinion.

Before we left the Ananda Saba, Swami gave us three big handsful of rice and a wad of 100rs bills. We all felt abundant before we even left. One of the local boys that comes to the ashram often to volunteer and could speak Karnataka told me to follow him. He was told to take care of me. Thank you, Swami!

When we got to Bidadi, my guide and I had just crossed the highway when a big shiny SUV pulled up to me and stopped. I was surprised to see one of the ashramites get out and put Swami's sandals down on the road at my feet and say, "Here are Swami's sandals. You have to wear them." I was astonished. I thanked him and tried to get my size 13 feet into the size ten sandals. I'm sure I could hear Swami laughing. When I looked up, I had a small group of ashram beggars around me with their mouths hanging open. They were shocked that Swami would share his shoes with anybody, let alone a Westerner. The boys told me a swami's shoes were sacred. Swami's sandals were a welcome relief for the soles of my tender Western feet. It didn't take long to realize that trying to keep Indian toe peg sandals on was going to take some serious concentration.

My guide and I started up the first street of shops. Some shopkeepers gave me a look that clearly communicated I wasn't welcome, but the obligation to give to a begging ashramite was too much for them to risk offending a swami. I began to realize that it was getting very crowded, even for an Indian street. Still, I was doing my best to concentrate on the phrase I had to say, "Bahgavati Beksha Deheem," and being careful where and how I walked, trying to keep the toe peg sandals from spinning around and out from under my feet. Then I realized one of the ashramites with the always-present video camera was filming me as I went from shop to shop. That's when I noticed that the street was not more crowded; it was just me. For some reason, I had attracted a big group of children following me around like the Pied Piper. There were about twenty kids following me everywhere I went. I smiled at them and then tried to ignore them. They didn't follow for very long, just enough to make me feel uncomfortably conspicuous.

After stopping at all the shops along the main road, my guide suggested we go to the next village just down the road. Being ignorant of distances between villages, I agreed and off we went. The toe pegs on Swami's flip flops soon rubbed off the skin between my toes, and my ability to endure the pain was reaching my threshold of endurance. We hadn't walked very far along the road when I saw a discarded flip flop in the ditch. I tried it on. It was a size bigger than Swami's flip flop with no toe peg. I thanked the Universe for answering my request to end my pain. I put the found flip flop on. My guide was stunned. It was unthinkable for anyone to take off a shoe given to him by his swami. How could I not wear Swami's flip flop? One foot was feeling much better now, relieving enough pain and concentration that I could focus more on my other foot enough to keep any more skin from rubbing off my other toes. After walking down the road for about six miles, I asked my guide how much further we had to walk. I was getting concerned about having enough endurance in the hot sun, walking along a paved road with no water. He just smiled and said, only 11 more miles! I stopped him and showed him my feet. Thankfully, he realized it would be too much for me and my tender Western feet to endure. He was disappointed that he couldn't go on but accepted his responsibility with grace, and we turned back. I'm sure he also realized with our size difference, there was no way he would be able to help me back.

By now, I was feeling beyond desperate for a drink. There was a small roadside cafe ahead on the other side of the highway that I had overlooked, concentrating so intently on my feet. Indian cafes along this road meant food cooked out front of an establishment on an open fire, burning just about anything, with a countertop nearby and tables and chairs in the shade inside. The place was constructed of cement block on a concrete floor with a flat concrete ceiling/roof. A rolled-up steel roll shutter hung over the opening where a front wall would be if the climate were colder. There were no doors or windows. The cafe was obviously popular judging by the blackened walls. Blackened from patrons leaning up against the unpainted concrete blocks sharing their road dust and sweat with the wall. In front of the cafe was a counter with deep-fried snacks and sweets for sale. The blessing for us was that most of these little roadside cafes had a 4-liter plastic jug of water for patrons sitting at the counter. We both gulped down half the jug each, Indian style where you just pour the water in without letting the jug touch your lips. Drinking this way seems to elude many Westerners, but today I made it work despite not knowing the source of the water.

The six miles back to the ashram felt like a hundred with painful blisters and skin missing from my toes. We stopped at every cafe along the road to share another jug of water. Somewhere along the road, I thankfully found another scandal that very nearly matched the one I had found, and it helped a lot with the pain. When we finally got near the ashram, we encountered a group of young boys who were aghast that I was carrying Swami's sandals and wearing obviously discarded sandals from the ditch. They wouldn't let me proceed until I put Swami's shoes back on. It was agony to walk the final 200 yards up to Swami's quarters to hand over the alms. As soon as Swami saw me, he beckoned me to come quicker. My arms swung faster, but my feet just wouldn't. I placed Swami's flip flops at his side and thanked him. Swami asked me, "Which was more pain, the shoes or the blisters?" I thanked him for the flip flops and gingerly knelt to hand over my alms. He laughed when I was getting up and told the group, "Karl got blisters instead of bliss!" In retrospect, the pain from the sandals was less than the pain might have been without any sandals. Swami fed us himself sitting on his porch outside his house. I was never more happy to lay down to sleep than that night.

Swami had taken advantage of people's reverence of a swami's sandals and provided me with his sandals knowing I would feel obligated to wear them, but also knowing I wouldn't know how to walk in them properly and would end up getting blisters. Was he punishing me for asking for shoes or just having a little fun at my expense? I got scolded from many people for a long time after for not keeping Swami's sacred sandals. I was just another naive Westerner.

That evening, we tried to do the fire meditation again. Shallow trenches now outlined our circles filled with the sticks and dried dung placed on top of the ground last time. The fires were even smokier. We brahmacharis called it the Smoked Brahmacharya Meditation. The fire-making process was getting better with diesel fuel soaking first, but still there was no heat after the initial flare-up. After a couple of hours of meditating while choking on cow dung smoke, we went back to the Ananda Saba for a short talk about how important it was to stay together to keep the energy high to let this re-programming work. Then we "slept" the night in the Ananda Saba again with Swami. There was a lot of sniffing and snorting by everybody to get rid of the dung smoke. The Indians here didn't clear their nose by blowing it out; they snorted it in until they swallowed. It was all very disgusting, but I suppose it is natural in a country with no potty paper.

Day 7 of brahmacharya training. Up at 5:00 am to clean up and be meditating in our circles of fire by 6:00 am. When the sun came up, it was hotter than the fire. After a few hours of fire meditation, we went back to the Ananda Saba to do headstands. We weren't finished until our combined time upside down equaled 10 minutes. The guys went first, then the girls. The young guys were laughing and fooling around. Swami said something threatening in Tamil and walked over to them and cracked the noisy ones over the back or legs with his cane. It was obviously not hard enough to stop all the goofing around. After breakfast, a group of photographers came in to do a photoshoot of Swami for promotional material. Our up-side-down class was suddenly less important. We took a break out of the Ananda Saba for a few hours.

Swami was just getting the group energy back by cracking a few jokes in Tamil about the boys' failed attempts at headstands when he called up one of the new acharyas (teachers) to practice teaching his first book with our small group as a test audience. To be an acharya, one had to memorize all six hundred plus pages of Swami's first book. The acharya was obviously nervous, and Swami kept correcting him, but it was all in Tamil, so I got a chance to catch up with my journal. Swami allowed three different acherias to demonstrate their teaching technique. All us brahmacharya students were nodding off. I was impressed by how much the acherias had memorized and recited.

It rained too much to continue the fire meditation that evening, so Swami told us now would be a good time to introduce his new meditation to the world. It would later be called Nithya Dyaan. It went like this:

Part 1 (7min) sitting on heels with eyes closed, breathe chaotically like hyperventilating, with short and shallow breaths mixed with long and deep breaths randomly to force the mind to focus on the breathing.

Part 2 (7min) sitting on heels with eyes closed, humming as loudly and as long as possible through your nose with tips of thumb and forefinger together on hips. Focus on the vibration the sound creates in the center of your chest.

Part 3 (10min) sit cross-legged, close the tips of the thumb and forefinger, and place palms down on knees with your eyes closed while being guided through a visualization of each chakra starting at the root chakra. Swami recites, "The chakra is clean and pure, the chakra is expanding," etc.

Part 4 (10min) sit cross-legged with eyes closed in an unclutched meditation (witness thoughts without attachment).

Part 5 (7min) Swami recited the Guru Puja Mantra for us.

Swami told us he would be making this new meditation a regular part of his programs. It is now on his website.

Sometime in the middle of the night, we continued the fire mediation. Swami instructed us to visualize ourselves completely engulfed in flame, both inside and outside, but with the cool of 1000 moons.

After the visualization, he told us the visualization was to keep our minds busy so he could get his energy in to work on us. I fell into meditation quickly and was visualizing all these flames burning me when the visualization took on a life of its own. The visualization expanded to a whole other level of vividness. I could see incredible detail right down to the intricate weave of my clothing's threads as it slowly burned off my body, revealing blackened skin getting thicker and harder without any fear. The thick black crispy skin started to crack. Brilliant bright blue light shined through each crack as the cracks slowly expanded. As the thick flakes of charred skin cracked and popped off, the brilliant white/blue light underneath became brighter and more loving with every piece that fell off. The light was blinding with the most overwhelming love I have ever felt. Tears were pouring down my face. I realized in that moment that enlightenment is not something you look for outside yourself. It is and has always been right there under the surface. I just had to uncover it.

There was a lot of charred black skin to remove to reveal my inner enlightened being. I hoped Swami would be up to the task of teaching me how to detach from my subconscious programming to unlearn who I am.

Day 8 of brahmacharya training. Too rainy to meditate in the fire. Head-standing again. I had no prior experience standing on my head, but with the wall's help and slow, careful moves, I got through the exercise. Today we found out that one of our ashramites is a famous Indian actress. She came to share her wealth of cultural knowledge in a very engaging way to make it easier for us Westerners to understand the Indian culture. She took all four of us international brahmacharya students aside to help us understand and appreciate what a tremendous privilege it is that Swami chose us to train as brahmacharis. Then she talked to me personally to make sure I understood how exceptional I must be for Swami to give me his shoes to wear on Begging Day. I didn't know if I should feel embarrassed or proud. She told us stories about how revered master's shoes are in Indian culture. After each story, she would look at us and ask if we understood. I was beginning to understand. The more I understood, the more I wanted to know.

Day 9 of brahmacharya training. We woke up in Ananda Saba at 5:00 am again. It rained pretty hard during the night. The roof leaked on my mattress. I had to get up and drag it to a dry spot. There were a few wet mattresses in the morning. This morning, it felt like I had a fever. The Ananda Saba is a sauna in the Indian heat with all the rainwater evaporating. After getting ready this morning, I was feeling better. A lot of our group talked about the heat and humidity. It must have been the energy. Today we all got the brahmacharya head shave. Apparently, shaving off my mustache made me look ten years younger.

Tonight we do a firewalk 40 feet long. Swami told another Westerner and me that we could not do the firewalk, that our feet were too tender. I agreed but secretly wanted to do it anyway. When Swami left, I planned to ask him as he walked by me, but he pointed at me when he left and said, "You get blisters from the road; the fire will be too much. Do not do!" No thoughts are private when in the company of a swami. There is no sleeping allowed after the firewalk tonight so that Swami can work his magic with our energy.

This afternoon, when we returned to the Ananda Saba at the prescribed time, it was locked with a person posted outside telling us that acheria training was in progress. We were allowed in after a few hours. It became apparent very quickly that our invitation was to increase the audience's size for the acherias to practice on. After another hour or so, it looked like we were going to get some Swami time, but a publisher came in and started showing Swami some book covers, CD covers, and other material. The publisher left, and our office administrator came in with a call that couldn't wait. Swami talked on the phone for a long time, or so it seemed after all the waiting we had been doing.

When we had our break, some of the young brahmacharis told me that I looked like a swami bodyguard now instead of a police bodyguard with my new skin-head look.

I talked to a young twenty-something videographer who came to visit the ashram today. He told me how jealous he was of us when we were in the fire circle meditations because of all the energy. He told us that Swami would make all the onlookers stand way back when we all got into meditation. Swami was waving both hands and shaking his hands over some people's heads. He said he could feel the energy from his position a hundred feet back. He thought we were all going to be enlightened right then and there. I was impressed with his observations. Usually, in meditation, there comes a point when you know you are done. I never got that feeling, even though we meditated all night long. The meditation felt blissful and the right thing to be doing, but it was not extraordinary this time. I felt like I was missing something. With all that energy, should I have been enlightened?

The firewalk was a shallow forty foot long flat-bottomed ditch with a twenty-foot water trough at each end. A fire burned continuously in the pit for half the day. It rained a couple of times, hard enough that we had to take cover, but not hard enough to put out the fire. When we were ready to start fire walking, all the big pieces of wood were pulled out with long sticks; all that was left was a deep bed of coals glowing intensely in the darkness. The glowing embers looked and felt much more intimidating in the dark. Swami sat at the end of the challenge. His instructions were to look into his eyes for the entire firewalk. It became apparent all too quickly that the fire pit was too hot. Water was splashed on the glowing bed of coals to reduce the heat. In my opinion, the fire pit was not too hot. The fire walkers were not instructed on the correct technique. The proper technique is not letting your toes bend, so they don't pick up embers when they flex back. Many of the boys got blisters quickly. One was still in a rickety old wheelchair 4 days later. Three girls were taken to the hospital crying and obviously in pain. At the end of the firewalk, I helped the girls into a car to go to the hospital when Swami called me back to receive my saffron shoulder wrap and sacred string as official recognition of my new brahmachari status. I consciously ignored Swami and finished helping the first girl into the car. I made sure somebody else was there to help before seeing Swami, who had waved and called me over a couple more times. I felt quite conflicted because I wanted to make sure the girls got into the car when no one else seemed to care, but I also wanted the saffron robe that symbolized my initiation into brahmachari. I recognized the same feelings rising in me as a child, when my younger sister got her foot run over by a school bus. I wanted to help her hobble home but was more afraid of what might happen if I missed my bus to school. This time, my sense of what was right demanded I help take care of the injured fire walkers instead of letting them hobble and cry to the car on their own. Another brahmachari told me later that while they were getting their robes, Swami said to them that the girls would all be fine. It was just a lot of drama. I don't know if that comment was chauvinism, another cultural idiosyncrasy, or I had unwittingly robbed the girls of something deeper. All I know is that I refuse to feel regret for helping when needed.

Day 10 of brahmacharya training. I put on my orange dhoti (skirt) today. It is quite comfortable, but going up and downstairs is going to take some practice. I keep getting my toes caught in the cloth's folds when I lift my foot onto something, like a step, and trip myself. I don't know why I should expect to wear a dress-like garment for the first time without embarrassing myself. Ego is still firmly engaged despite all my efforts to detach.

Swami says that we are going to his hometown today to parade around the town in our new robes and to see the temple. The 9:00 am bus didn't arrive, so another bus had to be ordered. It costs big bucks to travel across state lines. A last-minute request like the one we just made typically costs as much as an additional 16,000.00rs. Apparently, the biggest problem is that the government offices don't open until the agent gets there somewhere between 9:00 and 11:00. Our bus finally arrived at 2:00pm just as the lunch bell rang. We had a quick lunch before rushing off. The bus was about two-thirds the size of a Greyhound with less than half the power. We arrived at Tiruvannamalai Temple at 8:30pm. The temple closed at 9:00pm. This temple tour we were told to go fast, but with many of us with firewalk blistered feet, the group moved slowly enough that I could keep up. The temple was very hot, even at this time of the evening. We were all dripping with sweat as we waited in line. My new saffron dhoti was soaked.

To me, one temple was starting to look like another being sandwiched into a maze of passageways for hours with other devotees to view a small bronze statue for a few seconds as the line passed. Despite the temples' impressive construction, this temple looked very similar to other temples to my Western eyes. The deities were in small stone rooms/vaults the size of a small bedroom, about ten feet square with a seven-foot-high ceiling and an adjacent viewing room of similar size. The electric cooling fans looked like they had stopped working sometime during the Second World War. Everything was stone and blackened from centuries of coconut oil pujas.

As we left the temple, one of the organizers told me that this temple is one of five elemental temples. Each temple is dedicated to each element: earth, water, air, ether, and this one is fire. It was by far the hottest temple I have ever been in. Even the Indian boy's clothing was soaked with sweat.

Close to midnight, after the temple tour, we walked a few blocks down a dark village street into an equally dark unassuming doorway in the middle of a block-long cluster of dark closed businesses in the middle of town. The entrance opened into a large reception area for the adjoining Ashram. We were greeted warmly and led to a room where food was served in the traditional Indian style. We sat on mats with a part of a palm leaf on the floor in front of each of us. We had to sprinkle a little water from our cups onto our palm leaf and rub it around to clean it. Then we gently dumped the water off onto the floor. If you shake the water off, the delicate leaf breaks.

Eating off palm leaves is quite an honor because of the palm leaf's life force energizing the food. Servers walk around and place scoops of different rice dishes on your palm leaf along with various sauces. You either smoosh the rice into the sauce to get the right consistency or press a mouth-sized portion of rice into the palm leaf to make it stick together and dip it. Some eating idiosyncrasies are universal. Some diners must have all their food the same consistency. So the guy who gets too much sauce will grab handfuls of rice and sauce and squeeze it between his fingers until the rice is broken up enough to absorb enough sauce that all is the right consistency. Consistency is more important in a culture that eats with their hands.

Getting the rice to your mouth is simple once you get the hang of it. The method that worked for me was to scoop some rice up in my RIGHT HAND with all four fingers tight together. I used the tips of my now loaded fingers to rub the rice off the inside of my thumb. Then I moved my thumb to the back of the food and pushed it off my fingers into my mouth.

After we returned to the Bidadi Ashram, Swami called a meeting in the new food temple. He gave us all fire for how inefficiently the ashram was being run. There are a handful of adults and about 40 teenagers/young people. His admonishments were all in Tamil, so I have to assume the international students were not on his fire list?! He laid down the law and made sure that everybody understood they needed to have a job so that when he came back from his frequent travels, everything would be in order. The young ashramites were notorious for job avoidance, having little sleeping places hidden all over the place. I found one in the storeroom when I was cleaning it out. Another popular spot was in the mattress storage room. Swami wanted attendance taken at the 6:00 am yoga class and at the 7:00 am banyan tree puja. The next day, we were called to a similar meeting in the same place, but all Swami did was make jokes and generally put everybody at ease. Once again, it was all in Tamil. He surprised us with a comment in English that he is a compassionate mother and a strict disciplinarian of a father. The ways of a swami are as unpredictable as life.

Chapter 11

Living as a Brahmacharya

Day 11 of the 10-day brahmacharya training. Graduation day! It was initiation day. After another night sleeping in the Ananda Saba, the initiation happened this morning. We were all a little excited and nervous at the same time. Our three-hour morning recitations and meditations under the banyan tree were interminable while imagining what our initiation might entail. We walked in silence as we returned to the Ananda Saba. Cheering ashramites and visitors lined the path we walked to the Ananda Saba. We carefully took our places on the stage, arranged and re-arranged in our orange robes surrounded by brass deities, fruit platters, potted green plants, and coconuts.

As we sat waiting, wondering what would happen next, Swami silently entered and recited some Sanskrit verses and shared how proud he was of us all. Then he sprinkled blessed holy water on us as he recited more Sanskrit.

After his recitation was complete and we had all received a light sprinkling, he threw the remaining water over the entire group and soaked most of us. Then he cracked two coconuts together over our heads, splashed the milk on us, threw flower petals all over us, and blessed us with an Arati (fire ceremony).

Another brahmachari and I are the next level of brahmachari called Vanaprasthas because we have both experienced married life. There are four stages in a spiritual life, and Vanaprastha is the third stage where husband and wife vow to work with each other to help each other attain enlightenment. Functionally, we are brahmacharis. We don't have to carry the stick and rice bowl like the younger brahmacharis do. The final stage is Sanyas.

The brahmacharya program officially ended last night with a lot of music, dancing, darshan, and inspirational messages. During darshan, Swami blessed us with our new names as the brahmacharya training was an energetic death and detachment from our previous life. My new name is Sri Nithya Mokshananda, meaning eternally enlightened. I am delighted with my new assigned name. Some people need training to be able to pronounce their new names. All end in Ananda, meaning eternal bliss. It also means I must adhere to the rules that govern a brahmachari's life. the first being that I cannot talk to the opposite gender except those whom Swami deem energetically capable of communicating without creating any new samskaras or vasanas (hang-ups or karma). There are only about four people on the ashram that can communicate with both genders. It will be a lot of fun watching the few ladies capable of cross-gender communication run around like crazy trying to keep 40 people working with each other but not talking to the opposite gender.

My job is to work with the ashram yoga expert and create a yoga website together. The yoga expert is a younger woman, and there is a critical shortage of computers, so we all have to share. I talked with Priya today about cross-gender communication. She told me that after a year or two, we would all be brothers and sisters. Swami would then read us energetically to see if we were ready to talk to the other gender without incurring samskaras.

Eating oatmeal for the first time in this ashram today reminded me of you, Lynn, and your love of oatmeal. At this ashram, a delectable recipe of oatmeal is mixed with milk and sugar and spiced with cardamon and served in a cup. After all the Indian food, an excellent serving of something I can connect with home tastes great.

Today, Swami left for LA at about 6:30 pm. Everyone at the ashram held a big puja for him. The brahmacharis performed the puja on Swami's feet. He immediately got in his car and headed straight to the airport.

Someone in our international group quit and went back home to Guadalupe today. We had a meeting this morning and got instructions that we were not allowed to sleep. If we nod off, we must get back to work as soon as we wake up again. The program is now as follows:

4:00 am – morning washing and bathroom
5:00 am – laughing meditation
6:00 am – yoga
7:00 am – Guru Puja at banyan tree
9:00 am – breakfast
2:00 pm – lunch
9:00 pm – supper
10:00 pm – goodnight, swami deities puja

In between each scheduled activity, we are doing our assigned work. I am updating the Dhyanapeetam website, developing and designing a yoga website with Danika, which is complicated by not being able to talk to each other. We are also publishing whatever books need to be digitized for transmission to publishers.

Love,
Karl

My understanding of the purpose of the no-sleep rule is to put our egos into a state where it is so overworked that it can't police all our interactions, and from time to time, we should get glimpses of life without ego. Beyond ego is to function consciously without the habitual input of the ego. This is the goal of ascension and the whole reason for being here. Later, I learned that my moments of bliss-filled detachment are the true gauge of my ascension. Gradually, those moments of bliss become more and more frequent. At some point, detachment is your natural state, and bliss fills you because your ego waits patiently at your side instead of being front and center in your face.

Dear Lynn,

My last emails were more descriptive due to busyness and having to account for our time doing our work. I have some time today to be a bit more introspective. Before I came to India, I was so optimistic, I felt I might never leave India. As soon as I got here, I knew I wasn't staying. I have a strong pull to come back to Canada at some point when my ashram experience is complete to do what I can with what I have learned.

Today I got the crushing realization or liberation that I have no idea what might happen in the future. Side note, I have been operating on minimal sleep for a few days now. I sneak off to bed after midnight if I can and get up at 5:30 for Sun Salutation Yoga at 6:00 am. My "cold/cleansing" is slowly getting better. I miss my Western cold remedies. Another ashramite and I plan to sneak out of the ashram to get some Western food in Bangalore. I will get some Western medicine then.

Danika and I are respecting the "no talking to opposite sex" rule as much as we can, but we find ourselves cheating a little to meet deadlines. Even those in charge are telling us, "Go talk to him." There are not enough people in charge. Those in charge are grossly overworked and don't have enough time to deal with all their everyday responsibilities. Now they have the added burden of being the gender bridge for all of us needing to communicate with the opposite gender. This communication scenario encapsulates Swami's concept of chaos very well.

Communications start by calling out to our supervisor, on the other side of the room, the question we want to ask the person sitting beside us. The supervisor soon ignores us, and the one who was intended to get the message, sitting right beside us, answers as if the supervisor had spoken. It's all about rising above mind and ego. It feels more like being trapped in a nightmare of a bad comedy movie.

Living with artificially created challenges is nothing like my vision of what life might be like living on an Indian ashram. I expected days and days of meditation and silence. Instead, I am working in the most contrived, psychologically challenging way I can possibly tolerate without running away. We are not allowed to intentionally sleep, we have more work to do than a body could conceivably handle, plus the added layer of not being able to communicate directly with your work partner is pushing us to understand how ridiculous this whole endeavor called life is. This situation forces you into a dissociative state where your ego is no longer attached to your work's outcome. You work in a detached way going through the motions. It is chaos's way to get the ego out of the way and glimpse ascension. Not getting angry or go-for-a-walk frustrated in this contrivance is a huge new level for me. I am still waiting for my glimpse.

This morning, when I got up, my usual waves of bliss in my chest were particularly strong. I couldn't stop the tears from flowing for about 3 hours. It lasted all through yoga, up to the banyan tree, and all through puja. I got my glimpse! My throat chakra still feels like it is blocking full-out crying/energy flow. I'm working on that! I'm hoping things are grounding energetically.

Danika says tears mean the ego is working things out. On average, despite some profoundly moving experiences, I still really don't feel like I have ascended in my day-to-day interactions. The feeling of no change frustrates me and makes me want to come back to Canada. Three of the Guadalupe people just took off two days ago, and nobody knows what happened to them. The older one was leaving on a scheduled flight, and the two others planned to have an Italian dinner and return the next morning.

I talked with a fellow brahmacharya about living at Sai Baba's ashram. The place was beautiful. You had access to all the amenities, hot water, washer, and dryer. There was even a three-floored supermarket with all the Western food you can imagine. You didn't have to leave the ashram for anything, but you rarely got to see Sai Baba, and when you did, he was surrounded by thousands of devotees. The energy was nothing like it is here. There were restricted areas where only brahmachari or monks could go because of the energy. Life is much better here.

All of us from the international batch got a firing to today about how if we don't follow the rules, we are only cheating ourselves and all the work we went through in the ten-day brahmacharya training. We should appreciate the opportunity we have to expand. Just because we don't intellectually understand why things are happening the way they are doesn't mean we shouldn't trust that the master has only our best interests at heart.

Suffice it to say, there was enough guilt and personal grace to make us all resolve to keep to the rules. After all, it is only for another eleven days or so until the brahmachari energies have settled. We all sure hope the no cross-gender talk taking years to overcome will also be reconsidered!

Another ashramite is taking care of us for this week while Swami is in LA. She reminded us how Swami had talked a few times about how access to the banyan tree should be restricted to ashramites only because the tree's energy is being adversely affected by all the workshop people here for only a couple of days. I do feel lighter under the tree. I always thought the feeling came from being away from the business of the ashram and relaxing.

Today, a part of me is sitting here crying in frustration, while another part of me is saying, "Give it a chance!" It has only been two months. No doubt, being sick has something to do with it. A young devotee left a few days ago and left his cold medication, so I started taking that today. I have an infected sore on the outside of my right leg where it rubs on my bed's metal bars when I am sleeping. My feet hang out the end of my too-short bed because the beds are only six feet long, and I am six foot six. It is getting pretty ugly. My complaints about the problem are shrugged off by overworked staff. Swami's right-hand man, Rajananda, is a fully licensed doctor. He joined the ashram at its beginning three years ago. He looks kind of young, but I will see what he says about my sore. He came to the ashram in poor health. The medical community had written him off. Today, he is one of the key people who run this place. He also conducts several programs.

Lynn, I want to tell you not to come here, so you don't have to go through these challenges, but I guess that is all part of what it takes to get past the ego. I am told the ego is the easiest to get past, the emotional self comes next, and the final layer before enlightenment is the Being self. I don't know if I can hold out that long. I hope this is just a down day and things will pick up soon.

> The food is getting to me. The novelty of sambar and rice disappeared after a few weeks of repetition. Last night, we had dosas, thin rice flour pancakes. I put some jam on them that I had picked up in Bangalore. That was a heavenly change. Danika says there is no way they will let me install a Slurpee machine here! They have a washer and dryer that used to be available to the ashramites, but the young guys wrecked it. To their credit, they were village boys who had never operated a washer or dryer before. Now, only a few administrators have access to the repaired washer and dryer in a locked room. Mostly, they do Swami's clothes in it and all the saris they use for the deities and ceremonial preparations.

Love
Karl

This is the most depressing email ever. It felt cathartic to write, but I won't send this one to anybody.

Emotional turmoil, I am told, is a sure sign things are moving. Your habitual reactions do not work in such a dramatically different environment. You have to learn new habits, and when there are no habits that bring you peace, your ego gets dropped from the equation, and bliss is free to fill the void. I long for the day bliss fills all the space habitual behaviors now fill in my subconscious.

Dear Lynn,

This going without sleep is a big joke. Everywhere I go, I see ashram kids sleeping. They sit at the end of the library aisles on the floor snoring, hunched over a book in their lap. I go to the English Publication room, and they are sleeping in there. I go to see if I can use the internet at midnight, and the computers are going, but the girls are sitting at the keyboards asleep in the middle of their emails. Three girls sit with their arms crossed over top of whatever paperwork they were doing. Their heads are resting on their arms, and the only computer connected to the internet is being used by a bleary-eyed, massively overworked girl trying to catch up on ashram email that should have been responded to a week ago. This girl coordinates discourse transcriptions with volunteers in Bangalore, Salem, and anywhere else volunteers live. She also coordinates the publishing of the transcriptions with a Bangalore publisher who translates all publications into four different languages. She has an incredible workload, with an incomprehensible lack of social graces. Some make fun of her. Her voice sounds like it did when she was three. She never says please or thank you. She tells you when she needs something, regardless of you being in a conversation already or not, and she tells you to do things, whether it is her place to or not. She gets into trouble for her lack of grace and also for her lack of results. She tries too hard to get all the work done and forgets about everybody in the process. I am sure her manner is not intentional; it is just her nature. Swami likes to put her into departments that are running smoothly to shake things up.

It was explained to us this morning that we were to go into town for a medical check-up. We were supposed to fast until the blood test. Nobody told us. Priya admitted that she only heard this information as we heard it this morning. Danika, Petra, Pierre, and I could not go because we ate some bananas. My malaria medication required food to work best. After all the loud words, blaming, and hard feelings, it turned out only one gender was allowed to go at one time. The girls went, and us four banana eaters went into Bangalore for about five hours. It was wonderful! The freedom, the lack of deadlines, not having to worry about looking over our shoulders to see if someone was watching us talk to the correct gender or not. We all got to share our frustrations freely. Danika is really getting her ego bashed right now. Rajananda handed out some new mantras for us to memorize for morning recitations under the banyan tree after evening puja. There were a lot of verses in Sanskrit. He read one line and then asked Danika to read the next line. She diplomatically told him, "You don't want to hear me sing!" to make light of the fact that there was no way she would be able to get the pronunciation or inflection anywhere near correct. He insisted. Danika was wrestling with whether her reluctance to do the recitation was ego or a feeling of genuine humiliation at being asked to do something

Rajananda knew she would not be able to do., in which case, she should overcome her feelings of embarrassment and do it anyway to expand herself. In the end, she did the best she could. The worst part was that he accused her of not having enough devotion to attempt it. The accusation really got her going. Not only was Danika being asked to do something she clearly could not do, but she was told in a way that made her feel like a scolded child. We suspect we are covertly being trained to channel the information.

Apparently, Rajananda had ego issues when he first arrived at the ashram. Swami used it to push other people's buttons to help them get past their subconscious programming. If we were a little more enlightened, we would have seen the situation for what it was, but we lashed out in the context of all the pressures we were under at the ashram. Our egos felt vindicated. We were not feeling very ascended.

Love
Karl

Chapter 12

Bridges of Diplomacy

Dear Lynn,

We are all having trouble reading the Sanskrit verses. Our attempts to learn are fraught with contradictions and counterintuition. One of our ashramites told us that she had asked our ashram Sanskrit expert, Premalananda, for help, and our expert couldn't read the new material either. She typically reads new Sanskrit passages easily and has been told to correct Rajananda because of her expertise. Rajananda was belittling Premalananda in front of all forty of us students because she couldn't read the new verses. An expert from Canada said that the text looks like someone who doesn't know anything about Sanskrit attempted to transcribe what someone was saying. There are no pronunciation symbols. Words are broken into separate words that shouldn't be, and separate words have been combined into one long unpronounceable word. These verses are not Sanskrit anymore, and there is no way to read it!

Earlier this morning, Madeline went to see our office administrator about the Sanskrit issue. We call him our Public Relations Officer (PRO). He is a wonderfully warm and compassionate person who happens to live in the ashram. He called in Swami's personal assistant, who is actually more like his mom. Swami has been heard calling her mom on occasion. She is probably the most influential person on the ashram along with PRO. Both were very concerned. They called Swami immediately. Swami called Rajananda to the phone and gave him a firing. The result is that Rajananda had to restrain his ego and not treat international students like the Indian boys. With the Indian boys, he insults them and embarrasses them and then makes jokes in Tamil and gets them all laughing. Danika shared that Swami knows how much of a sacrifice international students have made to get here, and he doesn't want any more of us to leave because of how we were treated. If we choose to leave because this is not our path anymore, that is different. Swami doesn't want international students going back to their home countries and destroying the diplomatic bridges he is trying to build. This is the first time Swami has had any international students make such an extended commitment to his mission. We have to learn from each other. Bringing in a qualified Sanskrit teacher was discussed.

We found out later from Priya that Swami uses us, international students, to demonstrate how much devotion the Tamil students need to demonstrate. For the Tamil kids who are in their mid to late twenties, ashram life is easy. They come from their mom and dad's house to the ashram, where everything is still free. It is a colossal meditation adjusting to the ashram lifestyle for us international students, never mind going through all the ego-busting things that all the Tamil kids find challenging.

Swami's mission is to spread enlightenment. That involves attracting more international seekers to spread the mission worldwide, not to drive them away. In the end, Swami told Rajananda not to talk to us, international students. In our talks with Priya, she speculates that Rajananda doesn't have the life experience or skills to be diplomatic or sensitive to different learning styles. After all, he went from home to university to become a doctor where he struggled with increasing illnesses and came straight to the ashram three years ago. He has never known anything but Swami's methods. I forget that this ashram is still relatively new and working with a cobbled-together staff. As more professional people are attracted to the lifestyle, the ashram will evolve.

Tonight in mantra class, Rajananda was a different person. He spoke in English and answered our questions respectfully. He explained why he insisted we all attend yoga at 6:00 am. When he does not it is because he has dysentery and has suffered from it for 15 days now. He tried to explain that punctuality without reason is a method of breaking the mind, and mantras somehow are part of that. Then he excused us and continued to talk to the young boys in Tamil.

Some of the kids were weighing themselves on the produce scale. They asked me to try. I discovered I was 30lbs lighter. I suspect the result is from a lack of Western comfort food or a produce scale that hasn't been serviced since the turn of the century. I had never thought of Indian food as diet food.

Lynn, a note about what you might like to bring to India. I like my Birkenstock sandals, but the curved up edge keeps the pebbles in. Plastic flip flops are best when it rains. The locals tell me it shouldn't rain until next year, so maybe plastic is not a concern now. Velcro strapped backs are good because you do them up and step on them for around the ashram and then do them up around your ankle when you go out or want to walk fast. A flashlight is mandatory as the power goes out daily. I haven't used my socks since I took them off the afternoon I arrived.

There are tiny little red ants everywhere. The smallest little crumb will attract a hundred of them. Even a dead bug attracts lots. I noticed a few ants on my shelf one day and followed them to one of my Sesame snack candy bars still in its original wrapper. It had a tiny pinhole in the wrapper where the plastic fusing pulled a bit too tight. Inside the wrapper was a mass of crawling ants and sesame seeds. That package went flying out the door so fast there was a trail of ants in the air. Anything like cookies must be put into airtight plastic containers to keep the ants out. The drinking water here is from a reverse osmosis filtration system. The consensus is osmosis water doesn't quench our thirst. I drink it but enjoy it much better when I mix in the sport drink powder you sent me.

The next day was a medical check-up day. I was beginning to accept that many things in this country require more patience and acceptance about the way things are. Bussing with way too many of us piled into the ashram mini-minivan was my first post-realization test. Bidadi is only 10 minutes away but felt much longer in a van so close to the road its bumper dragged into every pothole and swayed ominously back and forth over the edges. Girls in one trip, guys in the next. We hopped onto the local public transit, which looks like a bus from the 1940s that just drove through a flower shop with half the flowers still covering the bus's front. The front 1/3 is for ladies only. The bus got crowded very quickly. It wasn't long before it was just one mass of hot, sweaty humanity. I was amazed as the "porter" managed to get around and collect fares from everybody, no matter how far outside the door the rider was hanging. Even those standing on the back bumper and hanging onto the back window ledge had to pay their fare. I hoped they paid less.

The hospital was a medical college, still under construction. The building looked like it had been under construction for a long time with piles of construction materials strewn around the place and rusted re-bar sticking out of the roof. We walked up beautiful stone steps through a modest wood door and down a short hallway that opened up into a huge waiting area two stories high where we waited for about an hour. The entire east end of the waiting room was open to construction still underway. A worker was blasting the ceiling in the new structure with a high-powered hose. The water was running through the waiting room where we were sitting. Nobody appeared concerned. The west-end of the waiting area was a beautiful big sweeping spiral staircase up to the first floor. The steps were six feet wide. It was good to have them so broad because there was no railing yet, and the massive window on the other side overlooking a beautiful garden two stories below hadn't been installed yet. Then it was off to give blood.

I got a couple of chapters of my book read while waiting again in the next waiting room in the blood laboratory. Priya was still prepaying for all of our tests. There were four tests for each of us, and there were about a dozen of us. The ECG test was 15rs, the X-ray 40rs, the blood test 75rs, including a 50% ashramite reduction. The fees were small, but the hassle of who to pay and where was enough that it took us all day. The ashram graciously paid for everything. The ECG bills were paid next, so off we went to ECG.

I took off my Kurta in the examination room. The bed I lay down on looked like the sheet hadn't been changed for quite a while. The operator squirted clear jelly onto spots on my chest. I was surprised at how much I was disconcerted when I saw the little suction cup things the doctor applied to me still had blobs of gel from previous patients. He had to hold a couple of the suction cups in place because they wouldn't stay. Three different times the examining room door was opened, and his nurse/assistant came in to talk to him about something. Not that I am self-conscious. It was about the fact that I was in clear view of all the men and women in the waiting room when India seems to be so conservative regarding gender segregation.

When the printout was in hand, he pulled off all the suction cups and dropped a cotton ball on my chest and said, "Clean up." The cotton ball was a bit like using a tissue to dry off after a shower. I used my handkerchief, an essential tool in a country that wipes water off with their hands. While I was still sitting on the table cleaning up, the doctor walked out and called the next patient to come in. I was still putting on my Kurta as the next patient was disrobing in front of me and being asked to lay down on the same table.

As I walked out of the examination room, I realized what feels so different about this place. Everybody is in street clothes. No uniforms or name tags of any sort for nurses or doctors. A few wear lab coats, but most appear to have just walked in off the street. You don't know who you are talking to or what their qualifications might be. I couldn't tell patients from doctors.

I went back to the huge waiting area to read another chapter in my book. Next stop X-ray. This time there were four of us taking our shirts off for quicker processing. We stood against the wall with our chests against a black film plate on a large metal rack, took a deep breath, and *click*—it was done in less than 2 minutes. They had to do mine again in landscape. At least there was no gel to wipe off this time. The X-ray machine looked like something out of the 1940s. Then it was back to reception to read another chapter or two in my book.

At lunchtime, we went down to the hospital cafeteria. The cafeteria is out the hospital's front door, around the side of the building, and down into the basement. I was told that hospital cafeterias are the best places for Westerners to eat cheap and relatively safe. It is open to the outside so the cafeteria can cater to the public, hospital staff, and patients alike. This cafeteria looked like something you would find in an inner-city high school. The floor was dirty marble, the walls were plastered over cement block, and everything had too many coats of paint. Stainless steel countertops were well used, a few stool tops were missing, and piles of dusty old surplus hospital furniture of all descriptions was stored against the walls and in front of the windows, so it was all a bit 1930s institutional green dingy. There was a small counter to order from, but I couldn't see a menu.

We unpacked the ashram food we brought. The only thing worse than ashram food, in my opinion, is cold ashram food in a picnic basket. They tried to make up for it by sending along chips and crispy things that looked like breakfast cereal, but they were spiced and salted like chips. Both were too spicy for me. All the Indian chips I tried tasted like too spicy curried chips. The chips labeled "American style" were the only ones I could eat. Thankfully, there was a small food stand just outside the cafeteria front door. I got a "Thumbs Up" labeled Indian version of a cola drink and other junk food. Good thing I didn't eat all that sugar before my blood test.

After lunch, it was off for more blood tests. I hoped the new tests were not for hypoglycemia. The attendant that took my blood was excellent. It was the most painless bloodletting I have ever had, but then he popped the needle off the syringe and poured a drop onto a slide while we were talking and used another slide to smoothly spread the blood into a nice thin film on the slide. Then to my surprise, he pushed my slide over a foot or so on the table to line up with the other twelve samples just sitting on the table drying without slipcovers. He poured the remainder of my blood into two test tubes labeled with a permanent marker right on the glass. None of the test tubes in the tray that he put my samples into had any kind of cover on them. All samples were examined and tested by a technician sitting at the same counter in the tight little room. One of the tests they did was for HIV. Apparently, it is compulsory. Back to the waiting room to read a couple more chapters. The floor was dry now.

The power suddenly went out. Everything was dark except the waiting room that was open at both ends to the bright sunlight. Most things carried on. They could still check my leg in surgery. The doctor noticed the big sore on the side of my ankle and asked what happened. He thought I had burned myself, but when I explained it was because the bed at the ashram was too short, he gave me firing and told me I shouldn't have left it so long. I didn't want to say I had been trying to get something done since I arrived two months ago. I didn't want to embarrass Priya too much. The doctor figured it out anyway and gave Priya a good scolding and told her to bring me back Monday at 10:00 am. If he didn't see an improvement, he would admit me until I got better. My foot was pretty swollen, and the sore was oozing. This is its normal condition now.

I found myself another bed as soon as I got back to the ashram, a regular non-bunk bed, so I could pile up three three-inch-thick mattresses for my feet to hang over the footboard without rubbing as I write this the next day with my foot up all day. There is no swelling and the sore is nicely scabbed over. I can put my foot down without stabbing pain. It feels a lot better. The doctor also put me on antibiotics and painkillers for five days. I am taking the antibiotics, but not the painkillers. The pain is mostly gone now. Maybe the antibiotics were for the examination room.

The doctor's assistant got me to sit on a gurney with a green rubber mat on one end to place my leg for bandaging. The rubber mat looked like it had seen a lot of different bloody patients. I could almost tell the nature of the injury because of the shape of the stains left by each previous patient. Gross! And this is a college where they teach doctors and nurses how to practice their profession!? Back to the waiting room until we are all finished.

Time for the bus. The bus we caught back was even worse than the one we arrived in! The bus's ceiling was about 6'2" I guessed by how much I had to bend my neck when I stood up. I was attracting quite a bit of attention and getting tired of it when one of the young ashramite boys grabbed my arm and directed me to a freshly vacated seat. The rest of the trip was much more relaxing sitting in a seat, despite all the pushing and shoving that goes on at each bus stop as people push to get off and push to get on.

We got off in Bidadi where our trip started and waited for the ashram mini-minivan to ferry us all back to the ashram. The ashram boys were told to start walking. After about ten minutes, the van arrived, and eight of us piled into the five seats. When we arrived at the ashram, we took advantage of the opportunity to talk to Priya. Danika shared her Rajananda experiences with her. Priya was very understanding and gave us some insight into the fact that Rajananda doesn't have the life experience or the understanding of other cultures or basically anything outside of India. He is working from a limited skill set. Priya told us that Swami is concerned about losing international students. He wants Priya and all of us international students to talk about how things could improve while maintaining the mission's integrity. After all, we are the first real group of International students who have made this kind of commitment to him, and he is expecting more international students in the new year.

The doctors at the hospital told her that something needed to change about what we were eating because every one of us, Tamil kids included, had diarrhea or constipation. It was about this time that the ashram mini-minivan returned with all the boys who had been sent walking. They were hanging out the windows, piled up on the floor with the sliding door open, all talking and laughing at once like a bunch of high school kids back from a field trip. The hospital was a refreshing change from our ashram life.

Chapter 13

A Spiritual Incubator

I am just finishing an excellent Western spiritual book I have read before. I needed a reminder of why I am here. My mind has been making it hard for me lately. No doubt, being sick, blisters on my feet, and a big sore on the side of my ankle had something to do with it too! I wrote a woe-is-me email a week ago, but I will call that one a catharsis and leave it at that. This big mutiny about how we international students are treated here gives me hope that some adjustments might happen. I can't go back to my life in Canada and pick up where I left off. It would feel like spiritual suicide. I don't feel any more spiritual now in my day-to-day activities than when I arrived. I get waves of incredible blissful energy that make me feel like crying every time I think of what I left behind and how little it feels I have learned. This is turning into another woe-is-me email. Suffice it to say, I am going through some stuff now like everybody around me.

I look forward to hearing about your swami experience in Joshua Tree, California. Did you take advantage of your time with him when he gave you darshan? It is tough to stay focused in his presence, and the music is much louder than I like.

Time on the single internet computer is so tight now that I have to write my message in a text file and save it to my USB key. When I finally get my turn on the internet computer, I quickly copy and paste my message from my USB key and email it. Then just as fast, I copy and paste any new messages I receive to my USB key to read when I get some time on the laptop. It is frustrating because I could more easily use the internet when nobody is there, but the library is always locked after hours now, and only one little, very controlling young girl has the key. She only speaks Tamil, and the ashram is trying to cut back on internet use because it costs so much. She is the perfect key holder. She treats friends and foreigners the same.

Love,

Karl

Dial-up internet on this ashram is the only option for low-priority rural farming areas, like this ashram. Each computer connects to its own UPS, and there is a big generator on the ashram to provide power during brownouts. Conditions that make ashram life a perfect spiritual incubator for emotional release are all part of the challenges.

Dear Lynn,

It has been a while since we connected. The phone I shared with Danika was stolen. I will get my own phone. Danika also can't find her passport. It's been missing since the second week she was here. Her passport was found months later in a book in the library where it appears to have been used as a bookmark.

Premalananda uses everybody's computer in the publishing center at the same time like they are all hers. Using ashram computers for ashram business isn't the problem. It is the way she does it. She comes over to you and says, "I have to use the computer," and she practically pushes you out of the way to do what she needs to do. If you see her coming and save your work and are prepared to let her do what she wants, you won't lose your work. She opens many windows on the computer, downloads all sorts of documents and pictures, gets what she wants, saves the download onto her USB drive, and leaves you to clean up the mess. Usually, all her messing about and removing the USB drive without exiting properly crashes the computer, and you lose whatever work wasn't saved.

One day Danika saw her coming and moved to another computer to continue her work, so she didn't have to deal with Premalananda. Premalananda came over to Danika's new computer and butted in anyway. Danika moved to a third computer, and Premalananda did the same thing again. Danika lost it. When Priya returned, Danika explained what had happened, and Premalananda just shrugged it off as a cultural misunderstanding. Danika tried to clarify that Indians sharing is not the issue.

Premalananda crashing the computers and causing the loss of hours of work is the issue. Premalananda never did accept responsibility for the disruption she was causing, and Danika was surprised she had such an uncontrolled outburst. She honestly thought she was beyond territorial issues, especially since she knew the computers were not hers. Premalananda's real work accomplished, chaos created.

The things I like to buy in Bidadi are fresh fruit and junk food. Priya tells me that now that I am an ashramite, the ashram buys everything for me. If I need toiletries or anything on their list, I fill out their form once per month, and I pick it up from housekeeping when it comes in. I haven't ordered anything yet. I'm still working on the supplies I brought with me. The ashram supplies me with three sets of all-white cotton clothes. Anything more is my responsibility. I have been living in two kurtas and two dhoti so far for the first two months. The ashram clothing purchasing system hasn't worked for me yet.

Things at the ashram are a little more relaxed now that Swami is in the US. We have settled into a routine that Swami will turn upside down as soon as he gets home, I'm sure, but the ashramites are getting the ashram spruced up pretty nice. The gardens have been all weeded. The garbage is getting taken care of every day now, hauled away and burned. A few construction projects are getting near completion, which means less dust in the air.

My new bunk mate and I are getting along well. Two girls arrived recently. They are the perfect button pushers to show me what I need to work on. One of them stayed in her room for three days because Premalananda butted in on her at the computer she was using and caused her to lose two weeks of work when it crashed.

I am dealing with disruptions better now that I have accepted that I cannot stay up without sleep indefinitely, even here at the ashram without guilt. I have been getting about three hours of sleep a night with a couple of naps during the day. When our supervisor asked about how late I would stay up to finish the science book, I told her until I felt sleepy, and she laughed and said that now I'm talking like an Indian. No specific time and total disregard for the rules, but not for ego's sake, for self's sake. Don't argue about a rule you know you are going to break. Just break it quietly without attracting attention. I'm looking forward to the three-month point in my stay here when it is rumored something magical happens to make life easier for me. I suspect one's ego gives up, and life goes more with the flow.

Danika just poked her head in and asked me if I was decent before entering my room. It is 10:15 pm, and I am writing this email on my bed in front of the window, which is actually a hole in the wall with metal wrought ironwork. I only have a dim red bulb on, so I don't think she can see more than my face lit up by the computer screen. Danika found out about a hotel in Bangalore that we could go to for Petra's birthday. It costs 46,000.00rs per night, and anybody who is anybody stays there. We certainly wouldn't be staying the night. She wants to go to the buffet, which is

500rs but is gymnasium-sized with absolutely every type of food you can imagine from star fruit and lasagna to sushi and desserts that a little-traveled Westerner has never heard of, including all varieties of cheesecake, of course. What is it with girls and cheesecake?

I am looking forward to your arrival at the ashram, Lynn. I am also concerned about how I will handle our issues when you are here. I hope to remain centered and witness my emotions, as I do with much of the drama happening around me now. Danika showed me a passage in a book she was reading that explained how a husband and wife have a unique opportunity over single people because of their commitment to helping each other ascend. And the fact that nobody can get at a person's issues like a spouse. Working out our emotional issues together will be intense but rewarding. I hope to be in better spiritual shape for both our sakes by the time you get here. Danika's book also explained that we are already enlightened. We don't need to do anything or go anywhere. We need to clear the programmed responses and the detritus we have accumulated over many lifetimes. Helping clear the detritus is what I imagine Swami's specialty is. I hope he has a big shovel for me.

All the people I have talked to here have been accommodating and supportive. There is a real family-like bond here, knowing we are all here seeking enlightenment. In the new year, the ashram expects a lot more international students to arrive. I am hoping for more than a few to add to the six of us remaining. I am concerned that more international students will change the comfortable trusting relationship we currently enjoy with our Indian hosts. Everybody is supportive of our concerns. They don't want the few of us left to leave. They want to understand our concerns and address them as best they can so that Swami can spread his mission and philosophy worldwide. Besides understanding how we relate to his teachings, he also needs us to spread his message. I am surprised, with what Swami offers, that so few Westerners answered his call to come to his ashram or, more likely, I haven't figured it out yet.

Danika has been talking with local Indian people who come to take her yoga classes. She says that this ashram is rough, even by Indian standards. It is commonly referred to as the crazy ashram because young people who run it have little or no life experience. There is often no place to sleep, and bathroom facilities are pretty rough, even by Indian standards. The comfort level is better if you are an ashramite because you get a semi-private room with your own washroom. Everybody else lives in a dormitory and uses a central washroom. The sound system and electrical wiring for small buildings used for classes is all just hanging from tree branches or other power lines. The power goes off regularly, and we get conflicting explanations about why. These conditions are Swami's chosen way to enlighten his devotees. We affectionately call this place the No-Star resort. Swami, himself, tells us his teaching method is chaos. Chaos is only one of many ways used to enlighten devotees. Chaos is the hardest but fastest way!

Looking forward to seeing you in a few months.

Love,
Karl

With all the chaos here, our egos have a hard time keeping up. It is harder to maintain our masks. Our triggers are more often in our faces, showing us exactly what we need to be working on. I look forward to the time when my triggers are nothing more than the ghost of a quickly fading memory.

Chapter 14

Like a Rock Star

Dear Lynn,

A few days ago, Swami took all us international batch up to the banyan tree and demonstrated the proper way to do a Homa. At unpredictable times during the ceremony, Swami would hold both arms fully extended in front of him and make karate chop motions over top of the fire pit and chant, "Fart, fart, fart!" For some reason, I found his chants hilariously funny. I was laughing uncontrollably. Despite the demonstration being all in Tamil, it was tolerable. English speakers were supposed to follow along in a few shared pamphlets. I found out later that "fart" is actually a Sanskrit word meaning to clear the air. How ironic.

The next day, all six of us in the international batch went into Bangalore to celebrate Petra's birthday. Her birthday is actually a few days later, but we scheduled the celebration to avoid conflicting with Swami's events. We went directly to the International Hotel by taxi for a smorgasbord brunch. It was a beautiful restaurant with a wide variety of fresh fruit, salad, sandwiches, and ice-cream. We were expecting to pay 500rs each as Danika's source informed us but were pleasantly surprised by a bill for only 160rs each. We all ate way too much! After lunch, we went to a nearby mall to shop for Petra's birthday present. The mall was a lot like any Western mall, which made us all feel a little homesick.

On the mall's top floor, some young people had created a haunted house in an empty store. It was, after all, a week before Halloween. I held the bags while the girls went through. There was a lot of screaming and banging. They all ran out scared out of their wits. Petra was so scared she was still crying, and her knees were shaking so badly she could hardly stand. While they were in the haunted house, I had my own fun. I leaned back on a big tree-sized concrete column to wait for them and unintentionally scared a few people who thought I was a mannequin. People turned and looked at me quizzically as they passed. A few did a quick double-take, and some jumped in surprise when I moved or said, "Hello."

Shortly after 4:00 pm, we got a phone call to rush back to the ashram as soon as possible to be on the bus leaving for Thiruvannamalai at 5:00 pm. We scrambled to get everybody together, all the time knowing that time in India moves differently than in the West. All of us from the mall got into the taxi. We raced off to pick up one of our group from the spa. Then it was off to get another one back at the International Hotel. We arrived at the ashram by 6:30 pm, and the bus hadn't left yet. We dropped our shopping in our rooms and quickly packed. The bus for Thiruvannamalai finally left at 9:30 pm for Bangalore, where we transferred to the Thiruvannamalai bus. We arrived in Thiruvannamalai at 1:30 am. By the time we all walked the kilometer from the bus stop to the ashram, found our rooms, found someone with keys to open our humble rooms, got the grass mats unrolled on the floor, it was 5:00 am. The musty rooms were built on the flat concrete roof. It was intensely hot and muggy, even at that time of day, which is normal apparently for Thiruvannamalai. The clouds of mosquitoes were relentless; thank goodness for my Kavi. I unfolded it off my shoulder and spread it over my entire body and immediately fell asleep. Now I know why my Kavi was made so much longer than everybody else's.

We were awakened a few hours later at 8:00 am. to discover the ashram was not prepared for us; apparently, we were one day early. It was a necessary diversionary tactic for Swami to avoid being mobbed. Breakfast was another kilometer walk across town. As we followed our host down the streets, the attention we were getting was a little uncomfortable. We were the international batch parade. Westerners dressed all in white with orange kavis attracted quite a bit of attention at the best of times, but a group of us must have been a rare sight for these locals judging by the amount of attention we commanded. People stopped whatever they were doing to watch/stare as we walked by. Children playing in the street would follow along behind us. We finally arrived at the private home of one of the people who helped Swami when he started his wandering as a young Sanyasi. In this typical small home, we were honored with our breakfast being served on fresh palm leaves on the floor in front of us.

Swami's other right-hand man (does that make him Swami's left-hand man?) told us that before Swami left this morning, he told the older brahmacharis that he built the Thiruvannamalai temple 3000 years ago, and the lingam in the temple is his grave marker when he was the enlightened master at that time. Furthermore, he planted the 600-year-old banyan tree growing in the Thiruvannamalai temple and that it is the same age as the banyan tree at his ashram in Bidadi; a third tree has not been found yet. Apparently, Swami sent his disciple at the time to plant the third one, so he never actually saw it planted, but it is supposed to be somewhere on Arunachala Mountain. Arunachala is the hill that overlooks the village of Tiruvannamalai. Legend has it that Arunachala is the embodiment of Shiva and home to Swami's third banyan tree. Just one more reason Tiruvannamalai is such a mystical place for Swami. The banyan tree at this temple and the one at Bidadi Ashram were DNA-tested and scientifically proven to be of the same stock.

We were rushed through our breakfast and hustled back down the road. We came in on to the ashram like a little herd of sheep to greet Swami, who was expected any minute. He didn't arrive until 4:00 pm. Swami went straight up to one of the rooftop rooms and called a meeting for all the organizers and, at the last minute, he included all us brahmacharis as well. There was standing room only in the cramped little space. Two fans were doing their best in the oppressive heat, but the sweat was still rolling off me like a good sauna. I was doing my best not to pass out from the heat and lack of oxygen. Swami conducted the entire meeting in Tamil, not a word in English. The rest of the day, we did our best to find someplace cooler to relax. At 10:00 pm, we were called to accompany Swami to unveil his new deity brought in from the deity makers we had visited on an earlier trip. We all rushed to get dressed, as most of us had retired to our rooms to strip down and sweat under our ceiling fans, desperately trying to cool down.

We met out front and packed into the small waiting cars. We didn't drive more than a few kilometers before we arrived at a devotee's house. We all crammed into a tiny little living room to look at a bunch of shiny deity ornaments. After a lengthy talk between Swami and the devotee in Tamil, we followed the devotee and Swami outside and into a large compound where we could easily see that this devotee was a man of many talents. In the courtyard, he had a couple of cows, many logs, lengths of steel, an array of sheds, and in the middle stood a five-ton dual-wheeled flat deck truck all covered over with taped-together newspapers. The devotee and a few others rushed over and ripped off all the newspapers like they were opening a big Christmas present. A beautiful mini temple was revealed. It was expertly mounted on the truck's deck, all ornately painted gold with elaborate cornices and decorations. Swami was beaming from ear to ear at the sight of this new traveling temple.

Three vehicles were arranged to shine their headlights on the life-sized deities sitting in the traveling temple. Swami climbed the stairs at the rear of the truck deck like a rock star mounting the stage to receive his award. The deity mounted in the traveling temple is Shiva with his left leg crossed over his right so his wife could sit on his folded left leg. Swami blessed the statues by pouring water over them, then turmeric, coconut milk, and more mixtures over them with many liberal splashings of water in between each. Swami sent us all away at one point so that he could energize the deities. Just before the sun came up, Swami finally said, "OK, go rest." Pierre and I took off and walked a couple of kilometers back to the ashram and were on our mats asleep well before the others got back.

Our thin grass mats on hard concrete felt like heaven. We felt like we had just laid our heads down when there was an ashramite banging on our door saying the procession was leaving, and we needed to rush. We rushed to get dressed and ran out the front of the ashram. One of the local devotees was waiting for us. He didn't let us stop. He ran ahead of us and down the street. I could see our Ashram banners waving in the distance. Were we going to run that far? YES! As fast as my sandals could carry me! We caught up to the procession just as they were entering the Tiruvannamalai temple. I was told by many people that I must take off my sandals before I entered the temple. I was paranoid about losing them in the thousands of sandals lining the sides of the entrance. I picked up my sandals and started to carry them with me. "NO"! Can't do that!" The devotee who ran with us took my sandals and put them under a table that a shop keeper was selling his wares from. All this sandal futzing made us lose track of Swami again. We were running again! The devotee took a wrong turn, and we were funneled into the public queue of tight, narrow, four-foot-tall, stainless steel piped, four-railed fencing, with a labyrinth of twists and turns that absolutely kept everybody in line. We had to push our way past the queued-up public, where more than a few people were not happy about letting us past. Our leader found an opening and called a guard over to get the gate opened to run in the wide-open exit lane. We caught up to Swami's party just as he entered the sanctum sanctorum to witness the first puja. As before, the heat was intense. Everybody was sweating profusely. The sanctum sanctorum was a claustrophobic eight-foot square. I positioned myself near the doorway for fresh air, but people kept squeezing in. When the last of our group squeezed in, I was right beside Swami sitting cross-legged on the floor of a 3000-year-old temple that possibly had his ashes from a previous incarnation under the lingam a few feet in front of me. All that heat was now feeling more like a spiritual supercharge.

I tried my best to keep focused on the puja to avoid being a distraction to Swami. While we received a front-row seat to this very special puja, the public was being ushered by between their stainless steel fences for a few-seconds' glimpse of the blessed lingam, but they were confused by a room packed with Swami and his devotees and the back of this big white guy's head (mine). Apparently, energies are concentrated and infused into the deity through ceremony and worship because we humans are not pure enough to hold the energy ourselves. As the devotees pass by outside the deity and glimpse it, they are infused with the love of God that has been infused into lingam. The length of time the devotee feels an elevated sense of God's presence in himself is an indication of his purity. We left when the Arati was complete. We exited the same way the public did.

A large group of devotees waited for a glimpse of a living Swami after seeing him in the sanctum sanctorum. Swami walked quickly to keep ahead of the crush of people. I was feeling a little light-headed from all the heat and energy and having a little trouble keeping up with sore bare feet from all the running. The younger brahmacharis did a fantastic job of crowd control. There was some serious pushing going on. One lady bent over like a football linebacker and shoved her way right through to Swami. Fortunately, she dropped to her knees at Swami's feet and kissed his feet and left before Swami even knew what happened. Harmless enough, but hard to walk with all those people trying to kiss Swami's feet.

Through the hot temple, we followed Swami to witness a few more sacred pujas and to help control the crowd when Swami stopped at unexpected points in the temple compound to give his respects to the deities on display. Every time he stopped, the group got bigger. Finally, Swami stopped at the temple administrator's office for about a half-hour before we made the final push for the temple exit. Out of the temple hallways into the open square, an enormous crowd had gathered to get a blessing from Swami. Despite our best efforts at crowd control, Swami was getting a little jostled. We did our best to get Swami to the back of his new traveling deity truck, where he quickly took refuge and disappeared behind the curtain. After a few minutes, the curtains were pulled back for everybody to witness Swami performing a short Arati.

When Swami got down off the back of the deity truck, the crush of humanity was enough to squeeze the breath out of you. All efforts to be polite and respectful disappeared in the crush of humanity. We only had to get Swami across the square to his stage, but it took all of us pushing for all we were worth against people who just wanted a simple blessing. I felt for the admirers, but the safety of Swami was our priority. Once Swami was safely on stage, we relaxed a bit. We all joined hands to make a human fence across the front of the stage and around his SUV in case he needed to leave in a hurry. Swami said a few words in Tamil and then sat back and watched an endless parade of all the groups that supported Swami pass before the stage. The sun was so hot, and we were not allowed to wear a hat. I was so thirsty. I broke ranks with bouncer duty and bought a bottle of water. As soon as I cracked open the bottle and had a few gulps, I could see the pleas of the other ashramites still holding strong. I passed the bottle on to the closest ashramite who was just as thirsty as me. He took a sip and passed it on again and again until it was gone. Those of us in line were sure the paraders were circling the block and parading past Swami endlessly to get energized with a living Swami's smile like a temple deity.

Finally, the parade ended. Swami got up, and we braced to hold the line for Swami to get to his SUV. Instead, he jumped off the stage, walked straight through our line, and through the crowd. Swami kept walking at a brisk pace down the road. He was circumambulating the temple. People were confused enough by his unpredictable behavior that Swami was making good time. It was a monumental shoving match getting through the crowd to catch up to Swami in the crush of confused people. It didn't take the people long to realize what had just happened.

We got to Swami just in time to hold back the swelling mob. After 3 or 4 blocks of trying to keep devotees respectfully at arm's length without hurting anyone and smiling blissfully, we settled into ranks and were holding our own. Every once in a while, a devotee would push another devotee at us so they could slip in the opening left by one of us trying to catch and push back. Our strategy worked well enough until the first corner at about the one and a half mile point when we all got ambushed by a coordinated group of ladies. We rushed Swami into the traveling deity truck that was now traveling ahead of us with devotional music blaring and whisked him off like a rock star.

The crowd moved along quite briskly after that for the next mile to get to the second stage. By the time we arrived at the second stage, Swami was already seated and ready to start, looking bright and fresh like nothing happened. A large crowd had already amassed. Another devotional parade passed in front of Swami on the stage for over an hour while all brahmacharis sat around the edge of the stage. Once again, without warning, Swami jumped off the stage. He walked briskly toward the ashram another kilometer down the road to complete the circumambulation. There was a considerable difference between the women's (left) and men's side (right) of Swami for us bouncers. The men walked on Swami's right side and were mostly cool, calm, and collected, but the women were brutal with each other and with us brahmacharis. They would try pleading, then pushing, and some would wind up and head-butt you, all while deftly holding a small child in their arms. Pierre told me he was watching from the sidelines, and it was such a frenzy that a few of the women ended up falling into the concrete ditches.

We finally got to the ashram that afternoon. We went straight to our rooms and fell asleep. It had been a full day, no breakfast, no lunch, and nothing could have made the day a fuller experience. We expected the knock on the door to be our lunch call. Instead, it was a brahmachari asking us to pack up immediately to catch the bus home. We were to meet in front of the ashram. Dreams of lunch vaporized as we rushed to get dressed again in our still sweaty clothes and out the door. We all stood out in front of the ashram in a tired daze. Nobody knew what was happening, where to go, how to get there or when!

Then the ashram mini-mini-van pulled up. The side door slid open to reveal space for two to squeeze onto the floor. Pierre and I took advantage of the propensity of the others to wait for instructions and loaded in. Doors slammed shut, and we were off. The driver stopped twice to ask for directions from people walking along the road. It took us fifteen minutes of driving to end up in front of the first stage where everybody else who had walked over was already waiting. Pierre and I looked at each other and said, "Ice-cream." That was all we needed. We were both hungry and tired, it was getting dark, and there was an ice-cream parlor nearby. We ordered fresh fruit with ice-cream. It was heavenly! The evening temperature was mercifully cooler, and from our new vantage point in the ice cream parlor, we could easily see what was going on with our group if we needed to move quickly. The deity truck and music truck were both parked in front of the stage. The music volume confirmed that either all Indians are deaf or prefer treble frequencies even more than Westerners prefer their bass.

The deity truck was lit up like a football stadium. The scary part was all the power needed to light up all those lights was provided by a cable powered by a generator pulled on a trailer behind an old 1940s era Willys jeep following the deity truck. If that wasn't bad enough, the power cord was held by a kid sitting on the hood of the jeep with the wire coiled up beside him to be let out or pulled in depending on how far away the deity truck got. The wire carried a lot of power and could have easily hurt so many people in so many ways. Amazingly, the wire made the entire eighteen-kilometer trip without any problems.

From our vantage point in the ice cream parlor, we could see the makings of another parade. After all the work being a bouncer for Swami today, the last thing I wanted was to be part of another parade. However, five kilometers along our parade route out of town, we saw a sign that read, Arunachala Circle Tour 13km.

Chapter 15

Circumambulation

Now that we knew what we were in for, we braced ourselves for a long walk and tried to establish a pace that would keep us ahead of the ear-splitting music. Pierre and I soon found we were so far ahead of the procession, we could barely hear the music. We slowed a bit, stopped at a roadside stand, and had a chai tea. There were many park benches along this famous road. Legend is that after one hundred and eight trips around Arunachala, you will be enlightened. This mountain pilgrimage is on the bucket list of many seekers, and here we were walking the route without knowing until the sign was in our face.

We continued our walk at a more leisurely pace. We came across a newly constructed bamboo framed building with a fresh palm-leafed roof and a big picture of Swami on the front. Another roadside tea stall a little further along looked like a good place to sit and drink another tea. We slowed our pace to a much more laid-back and comfortable gait. We were enjoying ourselves taking in the sights as we walked. The procession behind us ignored the tea stands and Swami's new building, and kept rolling on. The procession finally caught up to us. We sat and watched as many people danced their way past us in the temporary temple truck's brilliant lights. We waited until there were enough people between the trucks and us to buffer the intense sound before we joined in. It was very dark now under a moonless and cloudy sky. Arunachala was putting on an amazing lightning display all around us. The terrain was flat as far as you could see, aside from Arunachala, which is really just a hill. The lightning was truly spectacular. We easily caught up to the procession and got a couple of kilometers ahead of it. It started to drizzle, and my sunburnt head was grateful.

Apparently, it was normal for a light evening sprinkle in Thiruvannamalai. We enjoyed the light rain until people started commenting on how it was not letting up.

The rain was getting heavier, and the lightning was getting closer. Within half an hour, it was raining harder than these monsoon-hardened people were comfortable with. As the trucks passed us, we could see many people had jumped onto the vehicles. The vehicles had sped up, and all the procession people were running to keep up. Me and my tender Western feet were in no shape to start running to keep up. I just did the best I could to keep up. Within a half-hour, the trucks were out of sight, and we were in total darkness. Lightning flashes lit the road enough for us to keep our bearings. Pierre was feeling abandoned by the whole procession and was more accustomed to walking in sandals. He tried to convince me to hurry, but my sore feet could only handle so much. I probably could have just tightened my sandal straps in hindsight, and I could have easily moved faster. Pierre finally gave up on me, took off his sandals, and sprinted to catch up to the procession. There were quite a few of us stragglers along the way, but one by one, they jumped into buses and or private vehicles. Soon, I was on my own in the pitch black, with nobody in sight and rain coming down harder than anything I had ever experienced in Canada. I enjoyed the solitude, the cool rain, and nobody to compare with, nobody to keep pace with, just me, the road, and my soaked dhoti hiked up around my knees so I could move. I didn't feel abandoned. I felt peaceful. Somehow I knew everything would work out. As the road came closer to its starting point, I was passing more and more buildings and the most welcome occasional fluorescent tube light that passed for a street light. The rainwater washing across the road was getting deeper. It felt cool on my feet, but I also knew where the water was coming from—overflowing ditches of sewage. I got heckled in Tamil from just about every person I passed as they watched from the shelter of their porch awnings or open storefronts. The water washing across the road was about four inches deep now, and I could feel larger objects hitting my ankles as they rushed by in the water. I was thankful it was dark, and I couldn't see what was in the water. The buildings were getting bigger and closer together now. I felt like I must be getting close to Thiruvannamalai, but I had no reference. The water rushed down from the side streets in great torrents now. I was concerned I might step into a hole or worse, an open ditch, obscured by the flowing water. Then it happened: a dead end! Which way to go? Left looked just as dark and foreboding as right. Left was downstream, however. I lifted Swami's picture hanging from my Mala around my neck that he insists is his cosmic cell phone and looked him straight in the eye and told him I was lost and needed help! I spent a few more minutes there between frustration and visions of what my immediate future would look like trying to get back to the Ashram on my own. So much for the world all being right and all things working out! But then this fellow walked right past me between the steel posts in front of me, marking the street's end. The world was right again. Swami had sent me a guide! I hurried after him. When I caught up to him, he smiled at me. He spoke in perfect English.

"Arunachala does not give spiritual credit if you take the bus," he said. He was obviously walking in the rain by choice. The end of the road was the end of street lights and the beginning of an ominous-looking expansive slum. There was a maze of shelters built with scraps of whatever could be used for shelter. The uneven ground that passed for streets was impossibly dark. I was losing navigational reference points and was pretty sure I wouldn't be able to unweave my way back out of this maze if I lost contact with my guide. At this point, I was navigating by the shacks' silhouettes against the lights of Tiruvannamalai in the distance and the sound of my guide's feet ahead of me in the dark. Thankfully, the rain was letting up. We walked past two more laneways, another left turn, and the light of the entire procession taking shelter from the rain under a temple breezeway poured down the dark lane. The light filled my heart with gratitude at the sight of my goal and with pain as I got a clear view of the living conditions these shack dwellers survived in. I arrived at the parked procession as Swami was performing another Arati on the deities. I was surprised not to be missed. Nobody commented on how much later I had arrived. It was like everything happened in perfect divine time. I gratefully took advantage of Swami's Arati to rest. The rain had all but stopped as we continued back to the Ashram, only two more kilometers! The Ashram was as surprised to see us as we were to learn they were not expecting us. More diversionary tactics. They thought we would be in Bangalore by this time. It took a while to get us all back into our closed and locked rooms. I bunked in with the Tamil brahmacharis while they found my room key. The room accommodated four comfortably, six if you didn't mind being a little cozy. There were twelve soaking wet brahmacharis in this room. The one wire to hang our clothes on snapped when one of the hooks pulled out of the wall. We all just laughed and left the clothes where they fell. I was told to get out of my wet clothes, or it would make the grass mat I slept on wet, and nobody wants to sleep on wet grass! There I lay on half a grass mat between snoring brahmacharis in various states of dress depending on what was left dry from their backpacks they carried through the monsoon. Someone yelled food in the door, and they all shuffled out. I asked if there were any dry clothes anywhere. They said they would look. I waited. When they all came back after supper, they asked me why I didn't come down for food. I pointed to my briefs-only clad body, and then they asked why I didn’t put on dry clothes. I was getting exasperated now. We had left this ashram that morning being told we were getting on a bus back to Bidadi Ashram, so everything I had was in my backpack, and it was still dripping from the monsoon I had just walked through. They were shocked and very embarrassed. A few of the young brahmacharis rushed out and eventually found me a new dhoti, but I had to put my wet shirt back on. Of course, supper was done by then. I thoroughly enjoyed the not-so-spicy leftovers. When I finished my meal, the room I used the previous night was finally unlocked.

The next morning, we were told to have breakfast and get ready to go. When I went downstairs, something wasn't right. There were only six places set at a table, not on the floor like usual. There wasn't anybody else around. Not knowing what else to do, I sat down at the table. There was no way to ask my hosts, who didn't understand English any more than I understood Tamil. I was served graciously, all the while wondering where everyone was. When I finished and walked out onto the street, I found out that I had sat at the organizer's table, the organizers had eaten early, and everyone else was eating at the hotel next door! Out front of the ashram ready to go, I compared the menu at the hotel to what I had just eaten, and it looked pretty much the same. When we were all assembled, we walked the two kilometers to the bus station. It was an unusually quiet trip to Bangalore on the bus. The transfer to the Bidadi bus went smoothly. We arrived in Bidadi after dark.

As we left the bus, the driver called everyone together and told us we had to stay close together as we walked the last few kilometers to the ashram. I had had enough walking around Arunachala to last for quite a while. I jumped into an auto-rickshaw that had pulled up right in front of us. Pierre jumped in right behind me and another ashramite. As the rickshaw pulled up to our ashram eight-room-block, it was the first time the ashram really felt like home. The rickshaw's headlight caught Swami with four of his administrators like they were our welcoming committee. Swami and I had a pleasant conversation. It was a beautiful end to a challenging experience.

Love,
Karl

Dear Lynn,

Swami has decided we all need to be teachers of his book. We all quite enjoy reading his book and often get something new from it each time we read it, but to memorize an entire book is beyond my learning style. I couldn't remember children's nursery rhymes to recite to my children, never mind six hundred pages of an inspirational book. My mission now is to memorize as much as I can without any expectation that I can memorize anything. I am open to any miracle that might activate my currently dormant memorization genes.

Swami talked to all of us ashramites and told us if we wanted a more intense experience, we should join the acharya (teacher) training program. This invitation sounded a lot like the line that got me into this whole mess in the first place. I came here for a spiritual breakthrough, and so far, I wasn't feeling broken through yet. I signed up anyway. When in India, do as the Indians. Swami explained that the ten-day brahmacharya initiation was a symbolic death that severs all your earthly ties. The initiate is then reborn as Swami's child to be 100% dependent on him and his mission. My ego could never be 100%, well sometimes, maybe. I will follow the expectations as much as I can, such as being devoted to the master and his mission, working for room and board and not talking to the opposite gender because the opposite gender can be distracting depending on your state of mind or intentions.

In reality, not many of us follow the rules. Not in a defiant way, more like being respectful of the rules if the rules don't unnecessarily complicate things. As an example; yoga used to be at 5:30 am. Due to lack of attendance, yoga moved to 7:30, and now nobody comes. The ashramites have unconsciously realized their power. Organizers are trying karate in the morning now, but the instructor has so much ego, he is showing off all the time, performing such advanced moves that we can't possibly follow. He only lasted a couple of weeks. Swami's enlightenment method may be chaos, but even he gets frustrated when we don't follow the rules. Today he returned from a four-day trip to find out he had a birthday to go to this morning. He was angry; he didn't get any warning. We are all enjoying the irony.

Chapter 16

Acharya Training

Day one of ten days of compulsory acharya (teacher) training started with a three-hour lecture in Tamil. Ironically, Swami took the time to ask how many of us did not understand any Tamil; thirteen of us put up our hands. He commented that that was a lot. He continued his discourse in Tamil regardless. The frustration that typically arises when Swami doesn't speak English was tempered by the realization that I was a guest in his ashram, and this ashram's first language is Tamil. I took advantage of the surge of energy that welled up in me and refused to let the energy into my mental box labeled frustration. I enjoyed the undifferentiated energy as I just sat and experienced it. Needless to say, many of us English speakers enjoyed great meditations while in these classes.

Day two of acharya training started with a discourse consisting of one line: "Go talk to a tree!" Later on in the day, a group of ordained acharyas helped us talk to the trees. Talking to a tree meant to go and sit under a tree and study Swami's book. The group of ordained acharyas did an excellent job of motivating us and sharing their experiences. Still, in the end, it is up to us to be sincere enough to memorize Swami's six-hundred-page book well enough to make an accurate presentation of the book at some point in the not-too-distant future. There's that sincerity clause again.

Day three of acharya training started with one of our acharya trainers telling us that we should participate in Swami's Inner Healing workshop. After fifteen minutes of sitting in the audience with all the other Inner Healing participants, Swami asked, "What are you guys doing here wasting your time? Go study!" We went back to our trees and studied some more. No matter how hard I tried, the words weren't sticking. If someone asked me a question about something in the book, I could explain the concept in my own words. Not good enough. It had to be Swami's exact words as written. I still counted my explanations as progress.

Day four of acharya training. We found secluded spots around the ashram to study. I am loathe to create a prophecy to hinder my ability to assimilate Swami's book, but his book is his words, not mine. I am comfortable expressing his concepts in my own words. Still, the goal I am coming to understand is to consciously memorize as much as possible and then be able to channel the book verbatim from Swami's subconscious. Studying sure makes me hungry.

Day five of acharya training started with Swami calling all the English-speaking people together to outline his idea for three books he wants published. The ideas were mostly for experienced acharyas. We internationals were expected to share our uniquely English perspective and to make a mind-blowing contribution. In the absence of minds being blown, Swami gave us all an assignment to write a one-page response to what a stranger on the street might be told if asked, “What is Dhyanapeetam Ashram?”

Day six of acharya training involved a lot more studying. The best I could do was look like I was studying. The book was in English, but it might as well have been Arabic for all that stuck in my brain. Later that evening, during a meeting with one of the experienced acharyas, Swami walked in and took over the meeting. He told us that acharya training is compulsory. If we didn’t want to be acharyas, we should jump in the buffalo pond and go home! The pond was just a swamp thick with bull rushes and weeds where the ashram threw their garbage for regular burning. Wild dogs and snakes hung out there. I was tempted to go and jump in if for no other reason than to demonstrate how futile I was feeling about being able to memorize his book, but even the buffalos wouldn’t go in that swampy pond. It looks like I will be memorizing the book so I can stay in this ashram.

Day seven of acharya training started with one of our experienced acharyas telling us that acharya training is optional. I should go to the library and get back to building web pages. What a relief from having to jump in the buffalo pond. After that initial wave of relief, I started feeling guilty for not being able to help Swami spread his message the way he wanted. I'll work on accepting my limitations and be open to expanding my abilities when Swami expands my awareness. Does this mean my limitations are Swami's fault?

Day eight of acharya training is me taking Swami's book back to the library, throwing out the few study notes I had made, and settling back into HTML editing with a whole new level of detachment about all things ashram.

Day nine of acharya training and I am officially de-registered from training, but Pierre and Danika are continuing to study without the pressure of having to memorize the whole book or go home to see if they feel confident enough to make a presentation in front of Swami.

> Last day of acharya training, and Swami is gone to meet the President of India to invite him to his Jayanti (birthday) celebrations in January.
>
> Day eleven of acharya training is acharya testing day. Swami listened to whoever chose to make their acharya presentations. He didn't ordain anybody. Not even the one Indian woman who could recite the entire book verbatim. He told everybody to come back in three months.

Love,
Karl

I realize now that despite their desire to make this ashram more attractive to Westerners, their best efforts cannot change centuries of Indian culture. We either fit in or we don't. There is very little accommodation for our English language or the way Westerners learn. I am learning to accept how chaotic this ashram is operated, and I'm slowly realizing there is no need to change anything. It is the way it is for reasons beyond culture and my understanding. Either I learn to fit in or I find another path to enlightenment. Swami often tells us when he was wandering India in search of enlightenment; it was an abuse of a host's hospitality if anybody stayed for more than three days. Swami didn't travel the length and breadth of India by sitting at one ashram and complaining. Maybe it was time for this seeker to accept that I had learned all I was capable of at this point in my journey and move on.

Chapter 17
Salem Ashram Is Born

Dear Lynn,

Danika is planning to return to Canada in January. Two others have bought tickets to leave in a couple of weeks. At this point in my stay, life here is supposed to get easier. It doesn't feel any easier. Life on the ashram is still challenging. In defense of the life-getting-easier notion, I have noticed a growing feeling of indifference to some of the challenges here, such as when the laptop I'm working on screws up, and I lose my work. I used to chastise myself for not saving regularly enough. Now it is just part of life here, and I start again. The intolerant part of me wants to come back to a more comfortable, predictable life in Canada. The impatient part of me is concerned about the people who have been here three years already and don't appear any closer to enlightenment than I am. Finally, the eternally hopeful part of me doesn't want to miss anything. Failing the acharya training still haunts me even though nobody was successful. I didn't jump in the buffalo pond, and Swami didn't kick me out. Maybe it was all a sincerity test to see if we would run away. I will accept the buffalo pond as a challenge met and continue being hopeful. Maybe I am still hanging in there out of some subconscious fear of abandonment.

Swami says that he has cleared our karma from our past lives. Perhaps detachment is my life without karma, and I am only experiencing these fears because they have been entrained in my subconscious for so long. I have to teach myself a new way of responding to the absence of the old triggers.

Love,
Karl

Dear Lynn,

I am taking a short break from the ashram and staying at a friend's home in Bangalore. I am fascinated by Indian culture and the way people live. I can't help feeling that searching for enlightenment in India is so much more comfortable in a country that embraces and holds sacred the search. I have boundless respect for Indian seekers who renounce everything and trust in the Universe to provide for them. In India, the renunciate is called a sanyasi. In Canada, they would probably be called homeless.

Swami is pushing the publishing department to get ten books out before his birthday on January 1, which is in two months. He has been sitting in the library for hours, making sure everybody is working. The internet computer died, so the laptop I was using is the new internet computer. I have no access to a computer for personal email now. Swami usually sits at the end of the table the internet computer is on, so we can't even sneak in and copy and paste our messages while waiting for uploads to chug along.

Danika's missing phone was found in the field out in front of her room. It looked like someone carefully placed it there. Not a scratch on it and fully charged. We suspect somebody took it to help Danika work on herself.

All of us brahmacharis were sitting on the wet inclined ground for about three hours listening to him joke around with the Indian kids in Tamil. I have a hard enough time sitting cross-legged on flat ground, but this ground inclined uphill. My muscles all ached. I had to stretch my legs before they started cramping. Swami was a little taken aback and told me I could leave if I wanted. I thanked him and told him I just needed to walk around a bit. Our interchange broke the spell of his time with the young people. He told us the meeting was more about being in the energy than needing to understand what was said. He then wrapped up the “meeting” and sauntered away, leaving us all a little bewildered.

By the way, I am in the housekeeping department now. Changing our work assignments is part of how Swami works on us. When we appear to be comfortable with what we are doing, Swami will stir things up

> and move us around. Swami says those of us who have a high opinion of ourselves can have our egos broken like a dry twig. The challenge for him is those of us who are more humble because his attempts to break our egos is like trying to break a fresh green twig. It just bends. I am sure I am the latter, as my ego is always showing me how much more enlightened I could be if I were just a little bit more sincere.

Love,
Karl

I wish I could have felt the energy in that cross-legged meeting with all the young people the other day. We were sitting on the dirt road that connected the kitchen to the main gate for deliveries. There were beautiful flower beds on one side and small untended pomegranate trees on the other side hiding in the tall grass. The young people appeared to be having a pleasant conversation in Tamil with their guru with little concern for the rough ground they were sitting on. In hindsight, I must have felt something to have been able to sit cross-legged for three hours on coarse, uneven gravel. I was getting used to not understanding what was going on. I often practiced mindful awareness during these occasions to quiet my inner voice, and I sometimes fell into meditation.

Dear Lynn,

We were all invited by the Salem group to bless their land before they built their ashram. We left the ashram in a Tata Sumo taxi that took ten minutes to travel two kilometers down the hugely potholed dirt road to get to the mostly paved road to Bidadi to catch the night bus to Salem. In Bidadi, late at night, dusty, dirty yard lit by florescent tubes that buses used as a traffic circle, we caught a nearly empty city bus to Bangalore. The refreshing night air blowing through all the open bus windows was cooler and cleaner. In the Bangalore bus yard, we followed our organizers as they walked and ran, asking questions of anybody who might know which bus we needed to get on. We finally found the Salem bus conveniently parked in front of a small snack store and public washrooms. An attendant manned the restrooms. He demanded a rupee from everyone. I never did find out if the attendant was official or just someone who found a good place to beg.

The Salem bus was a pleasant upgrade from the hard city bus seats. Once settled into the nicely upholstered seats, people started nodding off. There were claustrophobic sleeping berths that tipped down from overhead. During the day, they doubled as luggage racks. The racks were so close to the ceiling that it didn't look like anybody would be able to roll over up there. Probably a good place to put young kids. Upon closer inspection, the sleeping space up there was obviously well used and very dirty. Curling up in our seats felt like a more hygienic choice. It was hard to sleep on the bus as it swerved around potholes, cows, and oncoming traffic in the wrong lane. However, a loud chorus of snoring suggested it was just me.

We finally arrived in Salem eight hours later at our usual devotee-owned hotel at about three-thirty am. We were let into our shared rooms with instructions to be in the lobby at six am ready to catch the taxi to the new ashram land. Most of us international people were prepared as requested. However, by the time everyone was ready, it was eight-thirty am.

The trip from the hotel to the Salem Ashram land was a long circuitous route through Salem's surprisingly green suburbs. There were some beautiful green spaces and many tree-lined streets. We eventually drove up a bit of a hill and wound our way through a forested area into a 200-yard wide saddle-shaped property nestled between two long ridges rising 30 feet above the property. The property is a park-like, twelve-acre mango orchard with neatly groomed flat grassland between the trees. Four families owned the property who then donated it to Swami. Last weekend, when Swami saw the property for the first time, he immediately fell into Samadi and never made it to the workshop he was supposed to conduct. An acharya took over the workshop, and Swami made it for darshan at the end.

The air is so fresh here on this beautiful property. It has a real peaceful feeling to it, like so many places in British Columbia. Devotees had a huge barn-shaped tent set up in Salem with lashed together bamboo and corrugated tin for the roof measuring about 100-feet square. The purpose of our visit was to inaugurate and bless the land for the new ashram to be built. Swami performed a Homa on a large built-up brick platform four feet wide by twelve feet long by three feet high with about 36 small Homa pits symmetrically arranged in front. Swami said that the new ashram built on this property is a seed for one thousand new ashrams and that we may not be able to see many cars parked here now, but from his spiritually attuned perspective, he could see the cars lined up for miles because there will be one Crore (10,000,000) people getting darshan at this new ashram. After his presentation, he started another Homa, which a brahmachari took over. The brahmachari struggled with the Homa a bit but did an admirable job. Lunch arrived in the middle of the Homa. Nobody was shy about leaving the Homa for lunch, which was a choice of a newspaper wrapped or a saran-wrapped serving of rice with curd or orange-colored rice. Even the people who like spice could not finish the spicy, hot, orange-colored rice.

After lunch, Pierre and I hiked to the top of the furthest ridge bordering the property to see what we could see. The view was spectacular. You could see for miles. It was especially striking because there were very few buildings taller than the trees, so the landscape looked like a forest of trees. There was a very distinct layer of pollution that didn't rise more than 100 feet above the ground, so the mountains in the distance were much clearer than they would be in the west. At the bottom of the ridge was a small neat little farm at the end of a road that led to a small village. Kids played cricket in the open grassy area between where the mango trees stopped and the jungle around the village started. The energy at the top of that little ridge was blissfully rejuvenating. There was a gentle cool breeze of sweet-smelling fresh air from the jungle.

We got lost in the sensations of this blissful vantage point for about an hour when we both had a feeling we needed to return to the proceedings. As we descended, carefully picking our way over the big boulders and around small thorny bushes, we realized things were too quiet, and the orchard was almost deserted. As we arrived in the shelter, so did two rickety old three-wheeled auto-rickshaw-pickup-trucks. The trucks had been sent to gather up all the remaining people. About twelve women squeezed into the back of one truck and a dozen men in the other. The old trucks looked like they were designed to hold eight small children, four sitting on each side facing each other. It was standing room only for the adults. Everybody held on to the sides, and away we went back down the hill, praying Swami was taking care of us. We snaked our way along a narrow dirt road through the jungle, back through rural Salem to the main road where Swami's now-famous deity truck we started in Thiruvanamalai was waiting for us. A couple hundred people gathered in and around the alleyway dancing to the deafeningly loud devotional music. They were all waiting for Swami to arrive to start the procession. Pierre and I took two others and went to get tea and snacks. We were still hungry from not being able to eat much of the too-spicy food served at the orchard. Half a block away in the cafe, we still had to talk louder to be heard over the music volume. After tea, everybody was still waiting for Swami. Our companions rejoined the dancing in the cramped alley while Pierre and I discussed our previous experience walking behind that very same deity truck in a monsoon around Arunachala. We decided to walk the few miles back through Salem to the hotel. We enjoyed seeing the city as pedestrians from street level. We half-seriously inquired about where we might get pizza at the hotel, knowing that pizza was an expensive luxury in Bangalore.

Surprisingly, the hotel clerk proudly told us to simply go down the alley to a place on the left. We were a little skeptical about going down a dark Indian alley, but the opportunity to get pizza emboldened us. At the other end of the not-so-dark alley was Salem's Culinary College entrance with English signs. This part of the college was set up like a bright and open North American food court complete with waiters. It was air-conditioned, neat, clean, and reasonably priced. The food was wonderful. Nothing special by North

American standards, but heavenly for Westerners living in a chaotic Indian ashram.

The next morning, in the hotel, eating a quick breakfast with the organizers, we discovered that the procession behind the deity truck yesterday finally started without Swami and slowly dwindled to a handful of people. The few remaining people jumped on the back of the deity truck and got lost until they accidentally ran into Swami. Swami led them back to the orchard property, where they did various jobs to prepare for the more significant festivities happening later that day. Sometime past midnight, they all fell asleep on mats laid out on the grass for people to sit on. In hindsight, the choice we made between pizza and working till you dropped was obviously the best, but it probably was not the most spiritually sincere one.

The next morning after breakfast at the hotel, we were taken to the orchard property by hotel taxi in time to listen to political speeches by too many politicians. It didn't seem to matter that the speeches were in Tamil. Without a doubt, Swami's speech outshone them all, gushing about how beautiful the land was and how many thousands of people will come to this as yet unbuilt temple. Swami then pushed the crowd back and honored all us ashramites with a beautiful palm leaf lunch.

There was an Indian version of a pinata. The pinata consisted of four fragile red clay pots hung in a row on a short stick suspended with a rope and pulley from the ceiling. Swami raised and lowered the pot and stick assembly as brahmacharis were called upon to try and smash the pots with the stick. Swami did his best to keep the pots out of stick range so everyone could have a swing at them. Finally, he let our youngest ashramite break them.

Pierre and I found a tea stand and took our time sipping from the minuscule plastic teacups. When we got back to the celebrations, most of the ashramites were running around in a roped-off area, throwing fluorescent-colored Duvali powder at each other. They appeared to be enjoying their unseasonable Duvali celebrations immensely. We stayed well clear of all the flying powders.

A big two-layered cake was brought up on stage for Swami. Swami carefully made a few cuts with the knife and then irreverently dug into the cake with his hands and shoved handfuls into the mouths of all the dignitaries on the stage with him. Dancing and louder-than-loud music started after that. Swami "got down" and pulled a few dance moves that got all the young people screaming like Swami was a rock star. When Swami had the crowd whipped into a good frenzy, he said that if anybody wanted to be an ashramite in the new Salem Ashram to sign up. The poor guy taking names was inundated. Darshan started soon after when the dancing really got going. Finally, after everybody went for darshan, Swami gifted a picture of himself to each person who committed to volunteering to be part of the new ashram.

Finally, after all the celebrations, and after Swami had time to leave discreetly, the hotel taxis started ferrying us back to the hotel. The

> next morning, eight of us went to the culinary college for an excellent breakfast before spending the next eight hours on the bus back to the ashram.

Love Karl

This trip to Salem was much more comfortable than other trips we had taken. We had a pretty good idea about what to expect and what was expected of us. We took advantage of Swami's absences to relax and sip tea rather than get frustrated. We found out later that hiking up the rocks surrounding the property to look at the view was foolish because snakes like the rocks too. We quietly thanked the Universe for taking care of us naive Westerners. We didn't feel obligated to participate in all the ceremonies and instead enjoyed taking some time to explore the area. It was beautiful, green, and lush.

At this point in my ashram stay, my wife Lynn had joined me. Lynn arrived the day before I had arranged to fly to Sri Lanka to renew my six-month visa. Before Lynn could settle in, we flew to Sri Lanka together. I suspected being a brahmachari traveling with my wife was probably not permitted, so I didn't ask. We had a great time in Sri Lanka touring all the country's beautiful history while we waited the five business days for my visa to be processed. When I returned to the ashram, Swami was not happy about my choice to travel with Lynn. Is it easier to ask for forgiveness than for permission? I continued to send messages to my mom in Canada.

Chapter 18

Consecrating Swami's New Temple

Dear Mom,

Now that I am a brahmachari, I had to move from my semi-private room with the bathroom to the brahmacharya bunkhouse. It is hard to keep track of personal effects in this ashram. The young Indian boys and girls have mostly come directly from their families in their villages to the ashram. The kids behave like this ashram is just an extension of their family. It is good they feel so comfortable, but they still expect someone else to clean up after them and keep them on task. One guy likes to borrow my little battery-operated electric shaver but has yet to return it. I ended up hiding it from him and telling him it was wherever he had left it. He never asked to use it again. All the male brahmacharis sleep in one big bunkhouse, and the women are in another. There are about thirty bunk beds in each bunkhouse. Privacy is a foreign concept here. I try to keep things in boxes under my bed. They stay there most of the time, but my wash bucket keeps disappearing despite having written my name on it in big black marker letters. I have a small 12-inch lockable cubical in a bank of cubicles that I have my lock on. My lock combination had to be handed into the office for security. Not sure how handing my combination to office staff makes anything more secure.

The most frustrating thing about this move is using the six public washrooms on the other side of the construction site instead of my semi-private inside bathroom three steps from my bunk. During regular ashram days, bathroom waits are not too bad, but the wait can be interminable during public events. Hot water is delivered by one heater (geyser) to all the cubicles. The kids keep playing with the heater, so the heater cubicle gets locked. The senior brahmacharis love having their own private locked washroom. Warm showers in the other cubicles have to coincide with the senior brahmacharis. Worst of all, there are only five washrooms left now for the rest of us and the public to use. Life here is our tapas (spiritual testing).

I went into Bangalore yesterday with two other Canadians. We were supposed to go to the nearby village of Bidadi, but we took advantage of our freedom and went into the big city of Bangalore. There is a Coffee World there that serves a heavenly caramel frappe that I can never get enough of. We had pizza for lunch, vegetarian, of course! It sounds like I will be going in again soon. The 600 rupee budget I was given for my shirt and pants set, jippa and pyjama, was wrong. I was supposed to get a higher quality set for 2000 rupees. I will keep the cheap set for around the ashram.

When I enrolled in the brahmacharya program, I was told everything would be provided, including all clothing. This is now five months later, and I am still patiently waiting for ashram clothing. The issue is my height requires custom-tailoring. I am quite happy to wear the cheaper clothes. From my perspective, this budget misunderstanding is simply the Universe's way of providing me with enough clothes so I can wash one while wearing the other. Swami plans on having us all on parade and wants us all to look like royalty. White cotton jippa and pyjama are as close to royal dress as this ashramite will get.

Our housekeeping boss is always screwing up his directions. He told us to take a single bed and bunk bed up to the two new rooms. When he saw what we did, he got upset and yelled that he meant an additional single bed to go with the one already there so that there were two beds total. So we just got upset back at him, and he admitted that he needs to speak English better. After telling him that he speaks better English than I do Tamil, he calmed down, and we both made a better effort to be clearer. Our international supervisor was transferred to a different department because we internationals were not behaving like we were supposed to. Rajananda is our new supervisor. I just had a heart to heart with him this morning. He is very diplomatic and enjoys a good debate. It's easy to see why he's so well trusted by Swami. He conducts many of Swami's workshops, and tomorrow he will do his first healers initiation. Swami will do the energy darshan, of course.

Rajananda illustrated my position to me by telling me that in the outside world, a person works for pay. Here in the ashram, people work for spiritual pay. He told me that the ashramite decision-makers are impressed with the amount of work I do in a day, but I have not collected my spiritual pay yet. He says I am still in resistance, and they can't get through. I was, needless to say, disappointed and upset because I had put my trust in the master to help me, and all this time, he still hasn't gotten through to me yet. It was supposed to be the previous supervisor's responsibility to help me along, and she didn't or couldn't. Rajananda promised me another meeting as soon as he could to help get things moving for me. I am happy that they are aware of my problem but frustrated that it has taken so long to get to this point. Entrusting my spiritual care to this master hasn't worked for me yet. If an enlightened being such as Swami doesn’t have the skills to get through to me, what else can I do? If Lynn wasn't here, I am pretty sure I would have returned to Canada from Sri Lanka instead of back to India.

Swami is pushing the “don't talk to the opposite sex” rule, which seems contradictory to his teachings that says if you make a rule not to do something, then that is all you will think of doing. The Indian response is, "How can you question the master?" in an exasperated aghast tone. Rajananda explained that talking to girls is like alcohol. It dissipates your energy. It helps to have Rajananda to talk to. We have been doing physical labor, which so far has been standing in a long line passing saucers of dirt, sand, or concrete along. The last couple of nights, it was concrete from about 10:00 pm to 2:00 am to build the new temple. The skin on my fingertips has worn off!

For me, as an ex-construction worker, physical labor at this pace is more like entertainment. I can do the work mindlessly and observe the frustrations of the young people trying to coordinate themselves. Saucers get dropped on toes, saucers pile up when two girls try to talk with each other, and people get saucers in the back. I try to help, but this group of Indians has real control issues. The girls more than the boys here won't listen to anybody. In the end, I just stand back and enjoy the drama.

The no-talking-to-the-opposite-gender is making life here more and more inconvenient as more people start respecting the rule. The sad part is that one of our female Canadians is a counselor and could be of genuine service to help people. I could sure use her expertise right now! I'll muddle along with my limited psychological tools. Right now, I am dealing with the no money requirement of all brahmacharis. Money isn't as big of an issue as not having snacks to squirrel away. We have a new chef again from further south where food is scorching hot, even for Indians. A lot of people are having trouble with the amount of spice. I used to skip dinner at nine and have a little snack, but that is not an option anymore now that I live in a bunkhouse with no privacy and nowhere to stash snacks. I anticipate losing more weight.

The language barrier is another problem for me. I see how the ashram operates and that it could be so much more efficient, but I can't communicate my insights to anyone. The ones who understand English don't have the mechanical aptitude to understand what I am trying to say, like our young twenty-something department head who only understands Tamil. I have mostly ended up doing mindless menial work because of that. I am enjoying being able to contribute in a more physical way, repairing things, filling the water cisterns, and moving all sorts of things without the responsibility of working on the ashram website.

In a meeting with Rajananda, he told us that Swami's vision for this ashram is the Osho model, where insiders are absolutely separated from the public. Apparently, at the Osho Ashram, the rules are absolute, and living conditions are much better. Not good, just better! He says it hasn't happened at this ashram yet because Swami doesn't have the people with the right talents yet. There is no female responsible and mature enough to take care of all the females independently of the males. Right now, the four male ashramites who have been here the longest take care of everything.

Our daily schedule is designed to keep us busy every waking minute with no personal time. It starts at five-thirty in the morning with yoga and ends in the wee hours with physical work. I have a hard time finding time to get my laundry done or anything else of a personal nature. I have a little time now because my housekeeping partner is sleeping with a fever, and I can't move the steel bunk beds myself. I seriously wonder where all this ashram life is leading. Some people came here three years ago when this ashram was started and are still not showing any signs, I can see, of enlightenment. Rajananda says I can't ask that question. Asking questions is how I learn and understand. It sounds like my faith isn't blind enough for this ashram. I will get answers one way or another, meaning I'll ask questions or synchronistically be in the right place at the right time to hear the answer. It will take more than just a little spark of light to overshadow all the other issues here. I have had a few blissfully enlightening experiences, but not enough to feel like I am operating at a different frequency. Hopefully, I will start getting that spiritual pay soon with interest!

I have to get this borrowed data card back to the publishing department. My data card repeatedly disappearing is another example of how this place grinds away at you. Ideally, it exposes your spiritual faults and foibles, but in reality, it causes frustration and hopelessness.

Love,

Karl, a.k.a. Moksha Ananda

P.S. I will probably have to give up my new Moksha name when I get back to Canada with the make-it-legal-or-lose-it requirement. I will see how I feel then!

I have since learned that my very low emotional state is my spiritual masters' goal. It is easier to be spiritually reborn without all the karma and emotional baggage that a normal life accumulates. I was being freed of my past behavior patterns to live a conscious life of detachment and bliss. I can't wait to experience detachment and bliss all the time!

Dear Mom,

After evening Arati at seven, we formed a procession of everyone on the ashram, about two hundred people, up to the new Anandeshwar Temple with lots of parade umbrellas, pomp, and ceremony. Swami performed a puja at the banyan tree behind the new temple then carried the flame to the temporary building set up beside the new Anandeshwar Temple with all the deities on display that will reside in different countries. There he performed a Homa followed by another procession back down the hill to the new temporary food serving area set up for the crowds expected for Jayanti, where Swami performed another Homa. We then followed Swami to the new temporary kitchen, where Swami talked to the ashramites and volunteers for a couple of hours in Tamil. Swami left, and the organizers took over. Department heads were announced, to great cheers and applause. All English-speaking ashramites were inexplicably excused from any departments and told to relax. Relax? We had just been fired from jobs we didn't even get hired for. We had no idea what was happening, and nobody was translating. I felt abandoned. I should have felt detached.

Later that evening, at about ten o'clock, Swami called all brahmacharis and Ananda Yogums up to the new Anandeshwar Temple to help move the huge Anandeshwar and Anandeshwari deities from the delivery truck and onto their new pedestal in the sanctum sanctorum of the yet to be built temple. We moved construction material out of the way. We cleared the area around the sanctum sanctorum, which looks like a twelve-foot square by three-foot-high raised stone platform with thick square stone columns at each corner supporting an impressive ornate stone roof structure. In the finished temple, the sanctum sanctorum will be the heart of the temple where the Anandeshwar and Anandeshwari deities are on display for rituals to be performed to and for admirers to behold.

When the crane, which looked like a backhoe articulated with a crane on the front, tried to move the first deity, it couldn't. After much inspection, the diagnosis was a broken axle. There were many ideas floated, or I should say, shouted. These Indians are not humble about how good their ideas are and why their opinion is worth listening to. The discussion sounded like a big angry shouting match. The consensus was that the crane could lift the deity, but the crane could not move with the load on it. The deity truck was maneuvered in close to the sanctum sanctorum with only minor damage when the truck ripped off a couple of feet of fake roofing from the truck. One inch thick boards bridged the four feet between the truck and the stone sanctorum. The deities weighed about five thousand pounds. It took a lot more shouting before one bright bulb doubled up the boards to make them stronger. Two boards are better, but I'm thinking there is still a significant strength deficiency for two one-inch boards to support all that weight. All attempts to move the deities by hand, rope, or pry bar failed. That much brass and steel doesn't slide on a wooden truck deck.

At this point, Swami casually sat on the deity pedestal, and the photographer seized the moment. The photographer directed Swami to strike many different poses, like a celebrity, on the pedestal. All work came to a standstill as we watched the photoshoot. Swami appeared to be enjoying the moment. A couple of hundred photos later, someone decided to push the crane into position by hand. The crane could still lift. It just couldn't drive. All of us pushed the crane into position. Finally, the slings were secured, the packing material in place, and a lift attempted. A few more adjustments were needed to correct the higher-than-expected center of gravity, but the next lift was a success. We got two inches clear of the truck. Now we all ran over to the crane and pushed it back away from the truck. Once the deities were clear of the truck, the truck got out of the way. We all pushed the crane back toward the sanctorum. The crane easily lifted the deity onto the platform, but the roof was too low to lift the deity onto the pedestal. The deity was unslung and the crane moved out of the way. While everybody noisily expressed their opinion about how the lift should be accomplished, another crane arrived. The deities were reslung from a lower point, packed with packing, and easily lifted onto the pedestal. The deities were finally installed on their pedestal at 3:30 am to loud cheering and claps.

Swami led all of us brahmacharis to the banyan tree and performed a lengthy Homa to the Shiva deity under the tree, then to the banyan tree and back to the Shiva deity again. By this time, we were all wondering what was going on because this was taking a long time, even for Swami. Suddenly, he put his hands on the top of the lingam standing in front of the Shiva deity and held onto the lingam for about a minute, then he put his forehead on the top of the lingam. Now we were all looking at each other hoping somebody knew what was going on. This process was new even for the ashramites, so we all curiously watched. After a few minutes, Swami lifted his forehead off the lingam and went over to the cave in the banyan tree. He spent a few minutes with each hand on the banyan tree parts that formed the doorposts at each side.

Then Swami returned to the lingam, put both his hands on top of the lingam for a minute before he called in the stonemason to chisel the putty away from the base of the lingam while Swami continued to hold on. After a few attempts, Swami finally worked the lingam free. Swami lifted the lingam free of the base and held it in front of himself. He reverently walked over to the banyan tree cave and held the lingam as far into the cave as he could reach for a few seconds, then held the lingam in front of himself again and slowly circumnavigated the banyan tree.

We all formed a procession as Swami passed around behind the Shiva deity, and we followed him over to the new Anandeshwar Temple's sanctum sanctorum and watched Swami install the banyan tree lingam onto the new base in front of the new big bronze deities. Swami held the lingam with both hands as the stonemason applied the red fastening putty to the lingam's base. With the lingam firmly secured onto its new base, Swami performed a lengthy washing and purifying ceremony where he washed the lingam with coconut milk, turmeric water, and kumkum water with much rinsing in between each wash. Then he performed an Arati to the lingam and threw flowers all over it. In the end, Swami spent an hour and a half moving the lingam from its pedestal, Avudaiyar, in front of the banyan tree Shiva deity to its new home atop a larger Avudaiyar in front of the new Anandeshwar and Anandeshwari deities. It was 5:00 am, just in time for the deity caretakers to start cleaning and dressing the deities for morning puja. They arrived as we were leaving.

Before moving the lingam, our morning Guru Puja was performed twice: once as usual, under the banyan tree to the Shiva deity and a second time in front of the new Anandeshwar Temple's sanctum sanctorum under construction. Now, for the first time in a month, the new Anandeshwar sanctum sanctorum puja was enough. Many people still like to pay respect to the original Shiva deity and hug the banyan tree after puja.

Love,

Karl

Chapter 19

A Blip on the Spiritual Radar

Dear Mom,

I am enjoying my unemployment from department duties. During my third time taking the NSP workshop, I had a daydream vision while discussing the "Chaos is order and order is chaos" DVD with Pierre. Pierre and I were taking the workshop to pass the time now that English speakers were not allowed in departments. I have heard this information before, but it is nice to get someone else's perspective. This time, the workshop was being taught by a fifty-something Bangalore banker. I am sitting in this class, trying hard to focus and concentrate on what he is saying. However, I still slip into a meditative space and experience little daydreams that are so real, it is only the movement of my eyes responding to some movement in my field of vision that snaps me back to this reality. In my vision, I clearly saw Swami sitting in his gated house transformed into a king of the world in his palace of light on a cloud inaccessible to mortal, three-dimensional human beings. Swami was looking out his transparent wall watching the interactions between the people in the ashram from high above. One of the ashramites struggled with the contradiction between what Swami said, "If you want to make a person dull, give them rules," and the reality of the non-compliance of the ashram's rules. The ashramite finally realized that both ways were right, and it was only the feeling of bliss in your heart that could tell you which way was right for you. At that moment of realization, the ashramite's heart center glowed brilliantly, and his perception of the third-dimensional world disappeared in a flash of white light. He rose up to Swami's brilliant world of light, and ascended!

> The vision gave me a bliss-filled wave of energy and the feeling that enlightenment may be closer than I thought.

Love,
Karl

This realization in my vision marked a turning point in my experiences at the ashram. I stopped being so concerned about being careful to follow Swami's contradictory rules, rationalizing each rule's reason for being, and focusing more on how my heart felt when confronted with a decision. If, for example, I was trying to decide between leaving the ashram or not, I would hold the image of how life would look if I chose one option, taking note of how my heart felt. Then I would focus on the other option and compare how my heart felt in that situation. The choice that made my heart sing the loudest was the right choice at that moment. My heart's song hasn't let me down to this day.

Dear Mom,

> The first day of Jayanti was ashramite's day. All ashramites were called to the eating hut at 10:30 pm the day before ashramites day. Swami organized us into brahmacharis,

Vanaprestas, Ananda Yogums, etc., so he could hand out new clothing for all to wear the next day. He got frustrated at the incompetence of the young people trying to organize themselves from his directions. He started whacking them with his cane when they weren't prepared. They got organized more quickly. The brahmacharis got nice new dhotis and expensive jackets. I got a less expensive jippa and dhoti that I had to buy myself because they couldn't find my size. And after a mix-up about whether I should get the jacket the brahmacharis were getting or not, the receipt got lost, and I could not be reimbursed for my jippa and dhoti. I didn't feel offended. I had witnessed the unintentional incompetence of these young people many times and knew it was not personal. It was Swami's chaos theory in action. Swami took ample opportunity to beat any brahmachari with his cane for almost any reason. It was hard to tell precisely what was transpiring because all the proceedings were in Tamil. Swami broke one cane over one kid's shoulder. It took until 2:00 am to receive our gifts and finally get to our beds.

After Guru Puja the next morning, we changed into our new clothes and paraded to the new Anandeshwar Temple, where Swami performed a small puja. We went back to Ananda Saba meeting hall where Swami had photos taken with each group: ashramites, brahmacharis, Vanaprestas, etc.

That evening, all the ashramites gathered in the Ananda Saba for some sort of initiation. Proceedings were all in Tamil! We internationals were used to being presented to in Tamil and not understanding a word. There were also some hilarious brahmachari skits. The brahmacharis started with the ashram music man doing a solo, which was pretty good, but the brahmacharis in the background doing an air band of the music was hilarious. The guy playing the violin was holding it like a cello. He was directed to hold it under his chin. He put it under his chin the wrong way around. He never did get it right, which made it all the more entertaining. After the music man's solo, the short lady sang. She was amazing. She was a singer by profession and chose a song that allowed her to display her talents' pretty broad scale. Then the air band moved off to the side for a fashion show. The MC told us that Sri Sri Ramashankar was coming out. A brahmachari came out dressed as Sri Sri Ramashankar. I don't know Sri Sri Ramashankar, but judging by the audience's response, he did a great job. He walked out from stage left across the floor into stage right complete with all the proper mannerisms and walking style. He did a great job and got a good round of applause from the audience. At one point, one of the older brahmacharis came out with only a diaper kind of wrap around his waist and a walking stick. All the women screamed and clapped loudly. A few more masters were imitated, and then two of the heavy set brahmacharis came out dressed in the diaper thing with only minor hoots and clapping. They were covered in verbooti and did a primitive dance with ash falling all over the place. Then they took a jump toward the audience and shook their curly-haired heads full of ash all over the place. The audience screamed and clapped loudly.

Rajananda came out as St. Francis of Assisi. The actions he made with his hands up in the air and gestures to come hither and be saved made the impersonation great. Next, the curtain opened for us to see our temporarily wheelchair-bound ashramite dressed as Osho, complete with the right hand gestures. He received a good round of applause. His real, full beard made the effect complete with just enough ash for aging. At ten years of age, our youngest ashramite came out dressed as Swami, complete with an orange robe and turban. Swami and the audience loved it. She held up her right hand and did a perfect imitation of Swami's gestures. Swami got up off his chair and went up to her and gave her his walking stick. The audience went wild with clapping and cheering. There were about a dozen "fashions" displayed, each worn by a different brahmachari portraying a different spiritual master. The show was a masterful distraction from all the Jayanti preparations and thoroughly enjoyed by all.

Love,

Karl

There was a story going around the ashram when the cane was being used on the younger brahmacharis about another enlightened master striking his brahmachari with his cane and severing the brahmachari's small finger. The result was instant enlightenment for the brahmachari. We ashramites suspected Swami was trying to enlighten his brahmachari, but we were not ready. The skits were a complete surprise for us internationals. We didn't know anything about preparations for the performances. It was one of the nice things about attending meetings in Tamil.

Dear Mom,

Our new international batch leader is very good. Swami appointed him as spiritual leader of the whole ashram. Our previous leader followed Swami's rules blindly, and when any of us asked why, she would get upset and ask us in disbelief how we could even think to question the master. Rajananda takes the time to explain why it is in our best interest to follow the rules. When Rajananda has finished his explanation, you are inspired to follow the directions for your own good! For example, when we go to Bangalore, the city is like an energetic speed bump. The ashram holds you in positive spiritual uplifting energy so you can grow, but a trip to Bangalore, like a speed bump, dissipates all that good positive energy, and it takes a while for the positive energy to build in you again. I feel more like staying on the ashram to allow the energy to do whatever it needs to do. If only the ashram had a caramel frappe machine.

All twenty-five of us international people are operating the new cleaning department under an ashramite that was in charge of the kitchen before. We are all cleaning everything everywhere. A few days ago, I was sitting in the library for one of our *Guaranteed Solutions* tests when I noticed a notebook lying on the table. The notebook was open to a list of points applicants should consider before committing to becoming a brahmachari. There were fifty questions applicants should ask themselves to discover how sincere their commitment is. We sure could have used this list before we decided to commit. I am not sure I would have made the same decision, which is probably why we didn't have this list before.

A few days ago, I had a great meditation at the banyan tree, where I very clearly felt I was with Swami. I took advantage of the opportunity of being with Swami and asked him how to drop my resistance. He looked me straight in the eye and said, "Just drop!" I placed both my hands on my chest in my vision and pulled all my resistance into a ball of light in my heart chakra. I pulled that ball of light out of my chest into the palms of my hands and laid the ball at Swami's feet. He gave me the typical Swami smile and wave, sweeping his right hand up and away like he was swishing a fly away, and said, "That's enough," and I felt a massive wave of relief come over me. I told Rajananda about the experience, and he grinned from ear to ear and said it was evident that there had been a significant shift in me, and he was delighted. I'm feeling a little more detached now. I hope it doesn't take another six months to get my next blip on the spiritual radar!

Love

Karl

Chapter 20

The Obstacle Course

Dear Mom,

This ashram is continuously under construction on multiple buildings. Many people are suffering ill effects from all the dust. Some have been hospitalized with lung issues. The dust doesn't seem to be bothering me except for making me homesick for a nice clean living space, a clean bathroom, hot water, and a little bit of privacy!

Memory tests happen regularly to determine how much of Swami's first book, *Guaranteed Solutions*, we can recite. The book is six hundred pages and is part of our teacher training to spread the message. Testing started with Swami saying whoever failed to commit his book to memory would be sent home. But when Swami called a meeting for the first stand-up-and-teach test and told us that we all failed, he changed the consequence to being tested regularly until we all passed. Only international people wrote the test, so when we rewrote the test, the Tamil kids also had to write it. We never did find out how the Tamil kids did or us either, for that matter! Every few days, we got another test. There is a big test on the whole book at the end of this month. The Tamil kids don't have to do the chapter tests, but they have to write the big one at the end of the month. I don't have a snowball's chance in hell of passing the test, so I go through the motions, hoping for a breakthrough and some new magical spiritual memorization power that makes committing six hundred pages of text possible for me.

Love,
Karl

Despite my impossible memorization obstacle, I felt everything would work out, and Swami would see the futility of trying to get me to memorize anything. We internationals insisted we were not here to become teachers. We were here for personal enlightenment. Swami said, "What to do?" and dropped the need to be an acharya. I learned later that Swami's pushing to memorize the book was his way of showing us how to learn to channel the book's material. In the future, the folly of trying to get acharyas to memorize or channel *Guaranteed Solutions* had to be acknowledged, and a computer-generated slide show was created to support teachers.

Dear Mom,

Yes! I still feel there is something here for me. Despite my ego, which is probably just trying to save itself, I will stay a little longer and make the most of what is happening here. My next big challenge will be not to have a stash of snacks so that I really will be 100% dependent on Swami. It will be good for my ego or not good, depending on how you look at it!

Construction on the ashram looks like a bomb hit the place. The entrance road is three times wider now. There is a huge pit where the fill was taken to widen the road. There are no barricades to stop cars from just driving into the pit. What was once a swamp is now a huge new dormitory with an eighty-stall washroom. There is a new road where there was once a swamp. Existing buildings are being enlarged. When they decided to demolish one building, they just evicted the twenty or so people. The evicted people had to find accommodation wherever they could. Most of them moved into the new unfinished huts. Doors hadn't been installed yet. They would often wake up with wild dogs next to them. It took Swami's philosophy of chaos a little too far. Carpenters hastily installed doors so the inhabitants could wake up relaxed instead of wondering what would happen if sleeping dogs were not left to lie. One of the new huts became the new school. I should say gurukul or school in the Vedic tradition. Vedic schools formed when a master in the forest was asked by children to teach them. The master taught them. In return, the students would take care of the master, and everything else needed to keep the group going. Grades one to eight here are taught in one seventy-five foot long building. Furniture kind of separates the three teaching areas. Besides the principal, there are two full-time teachers and a few ashramites who volunteer teaching. When I say full-time, I mean teachers wake the kids at 5:00 am to get ready for Guru Puja under the banyan tree. They hustle them up to the temple for meditation at 6:30 am, followed by Guru Puja at 7:00. At 7:30, the teachers get as many kids as they can to wash their clothes. Without Swami to supervise and no punishment allowed, wash time is like herding cats. After breakfast, school starts. The school day ends at 4:30. The kids are cleaned up, ready for 7:00 pm evening Arati up at the temple. After Arati, there is a little free time until supper at 9:00 pm. After supper, the teachers help the kids get ready for bed. In the beginning, the teachers were required to sleep with the kids. It didn't take long before the teachers got a room of their own to share. There are about 24 kids right now. Around the ashram, they sound like a lot more! We internationals are constantly amazed at how the teachers can get anything done, but then we only have our own experience with Western schools for comparison.

The Ananda Saba is getting a ninety-foot addition to expand the office, Galleria, and publishing program. The expansion creates some confusion because we have to walk through it to get to our bunkhouse and from the bunkhouse to the washrooms. A typical bathroom run, hopefully not in the middle of the night, from the bunkhouse, requires one to climb into the construction site through a large four-foot square window. Once in the construction site, all manner of obstacles littered in and around a typical construction site must be successfully navigated, including an unbarricaded three-foot wide by four-foot deep pit in the middle for the borewell. It is quite a meditation in the dark because you never know what workers did during the day. You might encounter piles of bricks, sand, cement powder, puddles, or even wet concrete. A part of me enjoyed the challenge of the obstacle course. I tried to anticipate what hazards there might be, based on what and where tools were and what was different from the last visit. Another aspect of me was frustrated that anybody would treat another person with such disregard that obvious hazards were not marked. Yet, another part

> of me was concerned for the safety of others that had to traverse the same obstacle course.

Love,
Karl

At five months, my six-month tourist visa was nearing expiration. Swami told us that a six-month tourist visa was enough as he could take care of extensions. I started doing visa research on my own time after five months to get the few reasonable airfares to Canada with only a few weeks' notice. I got into trouble for doing the research. Apparently, my research indicated a lack of faith. Swami said he would not take care of my visa until I surrendered more. That meant my bank account. The limited amount I had was already gone. There was nothing left to surrender. That made him happy. He promised to pay for all my visa expenses, and I had better get busy and complete my research. I gave the ashram public relations officer my research, and airfare to Sri Lanka was purchased. Lynn and I stayed in Sri Lanka for eleven days until the visa renewal process was completed. Swami did mention at the beginning of brahmacharya training that a necessary part of the training was to surrender your worldly wealth so that you didn't run away before his work was completed. Who you surrendered your wealth to was not his concern. There was more going on here than Swami attempting to put me into chaos. If chaos is all it takes to reach enlightenment, then my life in Canada as a public school teacher should get me enlightened in no time.

Dear Mom,

In talking to Pierre today, I realized that I am changing. When I get up in the morning, my mind chatter is noticeably reduced. After morning ablutions, I walk silently up to the banyan tree for morning puja at about 6:30 am. Sometimes in my morning walk, I realize my mind is completely silent. Of course, the realization of the blissful silence is my mind waking up. The more I witness my mind-changing state, the easier it is to return to blissful silence when meditating. The detached realization of silence is the next step to me being able to consciously detach from my ego and to be a silent witness to my mind chatter welling up without getting caught up in its unsolicited nonsense. There is hope!

Today, some of the young boys and I were supposed to remove the ceiling cloth from the three-story-high arched ceiling of the meeting hall, wash it, and replace it. Rather than go through the laborious task of climbing up inside the trusses and undoing the white cloth from between all the trusses, I found a long stick, tied a rag to the end, and wiped away all the spider webs. The ashramite in charge of cleaning, although amused, insisted the ceiling cloth still be taken down and washed regardless. The young boys had no trouble climbing up high inside the trusses to undo the fabric.

Love,
Karl

Chapter 21

Rules that Control What You Think

Dear Mom,

I have made up my mind to return to the real world, Canada, sometime in May when Lynn's visa expires. The longer I am here, the better Canada sounds. I don't know why I don't want to be an acharya. I like to teach people how to do things with their hands in my shop classes in Canada. Meditation, however, is not something I feel I can spend two days talking about, discussing, and facilitating. Plus, all the obligations and commitments one is subjected to being a benevolent missioner for Swami, and being sent on missions anywhere in the world hoping/allowing the Universal energies to provide. It is one thing for a traveler to beg for money or food, but to somehow come up with airfare, boat fare, or the means to cross oceans is beyond my faith. It sounds like my problem is not Swami; it is my faith in Swami.

My roommate and I enjoy a similar perspective. We are both baffled by how the Universe led us to this seemingly backward situation to learn how to move forward spiritually. We, two Westerners, are both suffering from culture adjustment issues. We know people here will not become Western to make us more comfortable. On the other hand, many people here have been incredibly helpful and treat us with more respect than many Westerners would have. In the West, a stranger might call you *buddy* or *sir* like they are a friend you haven't met yet. In India, a stranger is called *auntie* or *uncle* like you are family. It is heartwarming and has been very comforting in many circumstances, like the time I was lost in Bangalore. One fellow stopped to ask me a question. I couldn't understand his language, so he stopped another person who could translate English, and he stopped another who might know where my destination was. Soon, there were a dozen people all trying to get me to my destination. I felt so blessed and thankful when I boarded the correct bus to my destination.

I admire how Indians can carry on multiple regular conversations while ear-splitting music is playing. They can also easily take a phone call during that same loud music or on equally noisy public transit without putting a finger in the other ear. It is an Indian superpower!

I have been working out some of my aggression by play wrestling with a few young twenty-something guys when they frustrate me. Frustrate me because they do something inconsiderate or self-centered when we are all trying to live together in a small ashram. Wrestling with these guys has broken the ice and allowed the young guys to exorcise their frustrations with me as well as being as close to two guys in a Western bar beating the crap out of each other and walking away best friends as I can get - without the punching. It is part of how these guys relate to each other. For example, one guy had been turning on a little ghetto blaster full volume to wake everybody up at 5:00 am. I hugged him around the shoulders one afternoon way too tight and then grabbed him around the head and said something like, this noisy man will be quiet tomorrow. When I let go, he looked scared, but we laughed about it, and sure enough, the music the next morning was more peaceful, and he didn't come anywhere near my bunk on his wake everybody up rounds. We never talked before that, but now we joke and jostle each other around like good friends!

Pierre and I decided that the little glimmer of hope we are holding onto for enlightenment is probably just our egos. We signed up for one year, so we are going to tough it out for the year. The rituals have lost their intensity. We are just going through the motions. We feel like we have spent enough time and energy and have gotten all we are going to get out of this place. Maybe I should check out other ashrams. Others are expressing the same feelings. A brilliant professor from the US called it a lack of integrity. He said swami's words don't match his actions, which we know is all part of the process. The professor left after his first month.

I have become the unofficial Western welcoming committee. When I hear a Westerner is arriving, I prepare a bunk for them and greet them at 2:00 am when their taxi brings them in from the airport. They often have no idea if they are even in the right place. I have been told not to welcome new people, that arriving at a dark and sleeping ashram is part of the process. I continued to greet people anyway, and the ashram stopped telling me to stop. There weren't very many new Westerners anyway.

The decision-making process is changing. We are getting more and more rules and a council of ashramites whose job it is to implement and enforce Swami's decisions. Now we need written permission from the council if we want to leave the ashram for any reason. Most requests are denied. This is precisely the opposite of what Swami published in his book *Guaranteed Solutions*, where he says, "If you want to make someone dull, give them rules." Swami also says that if you want somebody to think about something, make a rule not to do it. Swami has put all these young people in positions of responsibility and decision-making for a reason. I suspect their positions are teaching them as much as we are learning, but it is frustrating sometimes when I just want an ice-cold frappe, and the young little twenty-something village boy says, "No!" I try to rationalize that the decision is for my own good to stay in the energy, but the energy hasn't cracked this thick coconut in six months. What can a few more months do for me?

Swami told us that his discourses are all just entertainment and distraction for your mind. You have to put the concepts into practice and experience it to get the benefit. I haven't experienced "it" yet despite desperately wanting to experience something lasting. I had an excellent talk with Rajananda. I expressed my frustration at being here for six months, and only now being told I am in resistance. I already knew that; it is why I came here. If dropping resistance was easy, I would have done it long before now. Don't expect to be able to just tell me to drop it when I have come halfway around the world at a significant cost to get some help. I have a sinking feeling I will spend the rest of my life trying to drop resistance. It is all rather depressing. I will email Danika and see how life after the ashram is for her. Her first email said she was so happy to be back home in Canada.

I did have an enjoyable couple of days recently. I was told to go around the ashram and to measure all the new buildings and digitally add them to the current blueprint file with auto-CAD, plus a few new buildings in the planning stages. Swami has plans for a huge swimming pool with a massive lingam in the middle of it. In discussions with other ashramites at lunch, we realized that if the pool is taken care of like everything else around here, it will be dirty and disgusting pretty quickly, and that will be the end of using it.

The pool was built as envisioned. It does have a fair amount of sediment at the bottom, but it gets used regularly. Nobody I have talked to on the ashram knows how to use the CAD software, so I hope to get more drafting jobs.

Temperatures stay warm at night now, which is scaring me because January is supposed to be the coldest month of the year. If this is cold, I hope I can handle April, the hottest month of the year! I feel a great sense of relief now that we finally have a firm departure date, but I am also open to staying longer if something miraculous happens, like my thick coconut cracking.

Love,
Karl

Dear Mom,

Today almost everybody in the ashram went to another swami's ashram to help set things up for his birthday celebrations. His ashram is in Kingery, about-two thirds the way into Bangalore. It is a beautiful small ashram on the top of a hill. It has a huge working clock tower. The tower is only telephone pole height, but the clock face is a telephone pole across with huge numbers and a sign that states it is the second-largest clock tower in the world! Good thing Indians don't exaggerate.

This morning we were told to be ready to leave for the Kingery Ashram at 5:00 am. All us Canadians were there at 5:00 am. We were all alone until about 6:00 am when a few Indian kids started arriving. We finally left about 8:00 am. As soon as we got there, we were put to work. We swept a huge temporary tented space, then set up hundreds of chairs. We put more chairs and tables for meals in another tented area. When I picked up a couple of tables from the pile of folding tables to set them up for food, the dozen or so volunteers started laughing at me. Initially, I assumed I missed another good joke. Then I noticed that it took two Indians boys to move one table. After seeing how I was moving tables, they all started taking one table each. So much for dropping my ego!

A lot of people came to this swami's birthday celebrations. The dignitaries arrived, and speeches were made in Tamil. Lynn and I snuck out and gave ourselves a little tour of the ashram. A banyan tree is at the crest of the hill with a seat high wall around the tree so that the area under the tree is flat. Around the perimeter of the tree are twelve small temples. Each temple has a likeness of the person or icon representing a different religion. The symbolism is beautiful. It is about how the tree unites all the various branches of religious/spiritual paths to the same source, the tree, existence. From the top of the hill under the tree, you can see miles in every direction. It gives you a feeling of being somewhere special. There is a beautiful little temple along the top of the ridge made with white marble and light granite. We walked up to the temple and weren't sure if we could enter or not, but we noticed some shoes at the front step, so we removed our shoes and respectfully entered. Inside, we saw the temple was wide open with a small room at the far end with a deity inside it. We also noticed one of our female ashramites sitting on the floor chit-chatting to a friend on her cell phone. She looked up at us as we entered and said, "I'm so bored!" After a few niceties, we respectfully approached the deity to see who it was modeled after and what offerings it had. We noticed the plate of fruit was not full. There were pieces of what was left of a pomegranate on the floor with a little red juice stain beside it, indicating that it was freshly eaten. Then we noticed two of our female ashramites fast asleep on the floor beside the deity with pomegranate-stained fingers. I wanted the mandarin orange but could not bring myself to eat fruit given as an offering to a god. We left the girls sleeping peacefully and walked out of the temple across the banyan tree area to the opposite side of the hill where a huge temple was under construction. It had five huge lingam-shaped spires about thirty feet across at the base and easily sixty feet tall. Three of the spires were complete, and the one they were working on was almost done. It was impressive.

We walked back down the hill and into the main entrance of the new temple. The ceiling inside was about sixteen feet high, with a large deity room under each roof spire. The rooms were all incredibly ornate with built-in drainage for ceremonial cleansings. The five geometrically spaced rooms in the temple space left no space for assembling, but they were nice separate rooms for doing pujas! The detail of the decorations was amazing. Three-dimensional circular reliefs decorated the ceiling, and many-tiered platforms were built up as the base of each room with many intricate carvings on all the rooms. The artists were at work as we walked through, creating these masterpieces. They looked like ordinary workers, but the artwork they were creating was masterful. We complimented them on their work. We weren't sure if they understood or not despite their smiles, and continued back down the hill to check out the main building.

The main building looked like it must have been the original building on this ashram. We were only allowed to see the main meeting room. One couldn't help but focus single-mindedly on the breathtaking white marble tiles. There were incredibly ornate architectural details all over, with a modest throne at the far end of the room.

At the bottom of the hill, lunch was a stampede! My orders were to be the bouncer and keep everybody in queue. As soon as we opened the curtain, hungry lunch-goers stampeded! There was nothing anybody could do. It took a colossal effort to wade my way out of the crowd and let it flow. Fortunately, the stampede was short and about the right number of people to fill the seats available. Synchronicity! The food was delicious, but once again, way too spicy for my Western palette.

Love

Karl

Chapter 22

Hyderabad

Dear Mom,

The international batch was called to a meeting in the library at noon by Rajananda. This was the fourth time he has called a meeting since becoming our supervisor. The first three times, he did not show up. We weren't expecting him to show up this time either. He surprised us all and showed up this time. He sat us all down in the library and started explaining how important it was to follow the rules again! He told us Swami himself would meet with us because the group energy was sufficient to make it worthwhile. Rajananda also explained that he wanted very badly to fire us because he felt so well connected with us. As Indians, it would be expected as a sign of closeness, but he knows that international people don't view firing the same way Indians do, so he struggled to express his feelings without firing us. After the meeting, Rajananda told me to stay behind. As the group left, three different people came up to him with issues needing resolution. Lengthy discussions in Tamil ensued while I sat patiently, wondering what I would be getting fired for this time. Finally, we were alone, and he told me that he had very, very good news for me. Now my mind stopped! Good news for me? Was it good news for him about me or really good news for me?

Rajananda said that Swami personally requested that I go to Hyderabad this evening. He went on to tell me that typically transfers of any kind involve a considerable amount of discussion among senior staff. Discussions can go on as long as two months before a decision is made. But this was a personal directive directly from Swami. Apparently, it was the first of its kind at the ashram. Rajananda hoped I was as honored in receiving the news as he felt delivering it. I hope I appeared honored because inside, I was reeling with all the possibilities of why he was sending me! I have heard the temple is beautiful with many fruit trees and gardens, but being twelve hours away with India's reputation for communication was not what I had planned for my last few months in India. On the other hand, I had to accept that I told Swami a few times in my quiet meditations that if he was going to impress me, he only had a few months left to do it. I think I just got my prayers/questions answered. As the news started to sink in, I wondered how I would break the news to Lynn. Rajananda said, "Remember, you cannot talk to women, so I will come by later and tell your wife for you." I had a hard time believing Rajananda would expect me to honor the no-talking-to-women-rule under these circumstances. I put on my best poker face and thanked him, and promptly left in search of Lynn. I couldn't find her anywhere, so I started packing. I knew I had acquired a few things since arriving, and I have had the feeling that I needed to go through the boxes under my bunk and get rid of anything I couldn't fit in one suitcase. Now it was time to give it up. I gave away more than I kept.

A couple of hours later, I connected with Lynn. Nobody had told her anything about Swami's plans for me. After the initial surprise, she decided that it was probably a good move, with the rules getting stricter and stricter. I was still mentally unprepared to let go of what little security I had being close to the Bangalore Airport. At 5:30 pm, I was given 750rs of ashram money for the eight-hour trip. With all my goodbyes said, an auto-rickshaw mysteriously showed up at the ashram to drop off a fare just as I was ready to go. Bidadi, here I come.

A short four-kilometer ride later, I was standing in the Bidadi bus terminal doing my best to choose from eight or so buses and a constant parade of buses stopping and going on the highway. Finally, I got confirmation from three independent sources that the next bus to arrive would take me to the Bangalore bus terminal.

My unofficial travel advisors at the ashram told me that I should always get a second opinion and a third if I wanted to be sure.

17rs and 35kms later, the bus dropped me off in the Bangalore terminal, and I was looking for anything that looked like a travel agent. I walked up to the HELP desk, and after trying to explain myself to the clerk a second time and getting the same blank stare, a guy grabbed my arm from behind and said he could help me. He led me out of the bus terminal around the corner about a block down a narrow back street to a small hole-in-the-wall travel agency. I was more than a little skeptical but had no other choices or offers, so I paid the 450rs fare, which included a guide to get to the bus. The guide, a young boy, was definitely needed as we walked at least a kilometer through back alleys, between shops that didn't look like they had a between, and across two highways to find a bus parked in the middle of nowhere at a curb under an overhead highway in front of a long concrete wall of some construction project. As soon as we could see the bus, my guide stopped, pointed to the bus, and asked me for a 50rs tip. I gave him 30. There were no signs or apparent reason why a bus should be parked there. Skepticism was in full force as I continued toward the bus. My guide had deserted me, running back the way he came. The thought crossed my mind that if this was not the bus to my new ashram in the village of Shamshabad, there was no way I was going to be able to find my way back to that travel agent! As I approached the bus, it was apparent the travel agent had called ahead, and they were expecting me. I got on the bus and started quietly asking a few of the passengers where the bus was going. After three confirmations, I relaxed into my numbered seat with my backpack on the floor beside me. I moved from the window to the aisle for more legroom. Good thing I did because the guy who took the window seat came handcuffed to a not-so-brief briefcase. He put the briefcase on the seat and then sat cross-legged on top of it. He then chained the briefcase to the seat in front of him. He spent the entire trip sitting on his briefcase.

This bus was called a semi-sleeper because the seats only reclined a little. It was like dominoes. Once somebody decided they wanted to recline, everybody did, or you had the guy in front of you snoring under your chin. I had to fight back feelings of claustrophobia a few times. At 8:30 pm, the bus left for Hyderabad. A movie started playing on the monitors on the bus. I'm glad I had my earplugs with me. All the movies I have seen on Indian buses are musicals with more dancing and singing than plot. The driver stopped at a few coffee shops; otherwise, I slept most of the journey. The trip consisted of the driver slamming on the brakes every once in a while with bumps big enough to launch you out of your seat and a few whiplash zig-zags to keep you from getting too much sleep.

Finally, at 7:00 am, the bus stopped in a little dust bowl of a village where the driver told me this was my Shamshabad stop. By the time I realized the village was really Jedcherla, the bus was long gone. The smaller the village, the harder it is to get someone to speak English. Eventually, I discovered that Jedcherla is about 70km south of Shamshabad and I had to find another bus. 51rs later, I was on another bus on my way to Shamshabad. Two and a half hours later, I arrived in Shamshabad. I phoned my new ashram as instructed, expecting them to send a driver. There was no answer, and then whoever answered told me it was not far, and I should walk. Walking would not be a problem if I knew where to go. I hailed an auto-rickshaw. The third auto-rickshaw-driver knew which ashram I was talking about. The driver asked for 70rs but accepted 50rs. Once I paid the driver at the ashram, I had 90rs left. When I told the ashram manager, Tathananda, about the bus driver dropping me off in the wrong village, he just laughed and told me that is how they keep the bus system going around here.

Love,

Karl

Now that I am in an ashram five hundred miles from the Bidadi ashram, I returned to sending my emails to my wife, Lynn. She then forwarded them to others at home in Canada.

Dear Lynn,

This ashram is way out in the middle of nowhere. I am feeling some pretty strong feelings of abandonment, like I experienced long ago as a child when my father demanded I get out of the family car in the middle of nowhere in the dead of a northern Ontario winter. I am also curious about everything that is going on here. I look forward to understanding why the Universe arranged for me to be here at this time.

The auto-rickshaw driver dropped me off at the base of a long wide, gently rising staircase flanked by a thick growth of overgrown mango trees and rose bushes. There was an acre or more of neglected rose bushes and other flowers nearby. This is an oasis in the middle of an arid landscape. From the ashram at the top of the stairs, you can see for miles in every direction. The village of Shamshabad was a short walk. The temple grounds are overgrown with many varieties of trees and flowers. The guest quarters are in a walled-in extension of the temple, in a locked compound along the south wall. brahmacharya quarters are cement block buildings outside the guest quarters wall perched on the top of an embankment. Each brahmachari's room could comfortably accommodate two bunk beds. Washrooms are in a separate building beside the brahmacharya rooms with an open washing area and clotheslines between.

The first room was full. I was assigned to the next room. I was very thankful to have a place to myself after living in a forty-bed bunkhouse in Bidadi ashram.

This ashram is not really an ashram. It is a temple. A devotee donated the temple and the land around it to Swami and his mission. This beautiful temple is currently a training temple for brahmacharis to learn how to run a temple of their own. Our entire day here consists of operating and maintaining the temple and all the gardens surrounding it. If I could use my Western construction tools to prune rose bushes and mango trees, I would have this place whipped into shape in no time.

The green gardens around the temple make it look like an oasis. Outside the temple walls, the landscape is cactus and other thorny bushes too tough for the village women looking for firewood. Behind the ashram are a few acres of rough bare rock. Depressions are rainwater pools. You can't just wander around outside the ashram, or your clothes get shredded by the thorny bushes. You have to stay on the paths. The temple looks like it has been abandoned or at least not maintained for a few years.

I feel very isolated here. The temple boys are friendly enough, but only two speak English, and one of them is out with a bad back. All conversations are in Tamil unless I specifically ask something, or the odd time I am referred to in a conversation, someone will take a minute to translate for me. Even when I do ask questions or make comments, Tamil takes priority. I feel like I have been put into involuntary silence. I don't usually talk all that much anyway, but it would be nice to be part of the conversation when jobs get assigned and the bigger purpose is explained.

When the sun sets here, it goes through three distinct layers of atmospheric haze. The first layer turns the sun a distinctly orange color and casts an orange hue over everything, like forest fire smoke does back in Canada. The haze dims the sun enough that one can almost look at it. The second layer creates a distinct line across the sun, like moving behind a piece of tinted glass. This layer is about three sun diameters above the horizon and turns the sun a beautiful deep reddish-orange and is mesmerizingly beautiful to look at. The third and last layer is about one sun diameter above the horizon and is so thick that the sun actually sets into this layer instead of behind the horizon. It is scary to think about how much pollution it takes to completely blot out the sun like that. I don't even want to think about what I might be breathing.

Tathananda took us all to the Hyderabad Zoo Park. It is huge. For 200rs, you can drive your car in with a maximum of 5 people inside. The zoo was relatively well maintained compared to the rest of the city. Most of the exhibits were in natural settings surrounded by a moat and then a brick wall. Many habitats looked neglected. Water was covered in green scum, plants and grass were scarce. The habitats looked overused. When I made a comment to Tathananda about the conditions, he said, "What! It is good enough for these fellows!" We went on a mini safari in a 20-passenger bus with 30 people in it. The safari bus wound its way through a few natural ten-acre habitats, each with high fencing and thick foliage. The bear habitat had large man-made caves that acted as a wall from the rest of the zoo. Two bears were fighting right in the middle of the road when the bus drove into the habitat. Access to each area is controlled with a large double gate so that the bus can be entirely inside before one gate is closed and the next one is opened. The bus had bars where window glass used to be. It was an interesting reversal of roles to have the people behind bars for a change. After the safari, we walked to the large lake that formed one border of the zoo. The younger brahmacharis were very excited about going on a speed boat trip. The boat looked like it was seriously underpowered by Western standards, but the 40hp motor was fast enough for these village brahmacharis who had never seen such a large body of water.

After waiting for the boys to have their boat rides, we walked through an artificial nocturnal habitat with blue lights inside, so the animals thought it was night time, but we could see them moving around. A few of the areas were separated with a curtain of small chains to keep echo-locating animals in their respective areas. Surprisingly, the bat habitat had no barrier between the bats and us. There were crocodiles and elephants, but no long-necked geese or unicorns! No humpy back camels, but lots of chimpanzees.

On our way out, our temple manager bought us all the first ice cream since arriving in Hyderabad's refrigerator-less temple. On the bus back to the temple, I felt a pang of homesickness when I saw a sign that read Bangalore 555km.

When we got back to the temple, we were all feeling pretty good. Tathananda took care of our good feelings when he stopped one of the brahmacharis from going back to his room to rest. Tathananda told all of us that we should only go to our room to die, meaning we should be so tired that we cannot even make it back to our rooms to die. We should just fall down and have a short nap until we awaken, then get up and get back to work. We were all reassigned to new jobs. Tathananda assigned me the morning dressing of the deity and Guru Puja. I was to watch others a few times and then take over. The dressing should be easy, but chanting 45 minutes of mantras will be a challenge.

It looks like my reason for being here is to learn how to run an ashram to set up my own center in Canada. Tathananda keeps making comments to that effect. I will do my best to pick up what I can, but I can't imagine any Westerner reciting Sanskrit verses to a brass deity. I had hoped I could talk to Tathananda, but he is so black and white about anything to do with swami that I just get swami-talk back in my face at the slightest hint of being less than 100% sincere. He believes he is a swami himself. If people converse with him about life, he immediately interrupts them and asks for their help with his mission. If they don't respond positively, he walks away. Tathananda has shared some interesting stories about his youth in Hyderabad with me. He can be such a nice guy until that swami switch is flipped.

> The bedrock is exposed behind the temple to reveal a few natural pools of beautiful clear water about 15 to 20 feet deep by 50 to 70 feet across. There are eight large lingams placed around the area. I could not discern any pattern. When I asked Tathananda about them, he laughed and said that many people, homeless and otherwise, would use the pools for a bathroom and cow wash. The temple smelled intolerably bad; when the wind blew the wrong way it was nauseating. With the newly installed lingams, no one would dare use the area because a swami has blessed it. Tathananda also said that it is government land, and the lingams can prove that we have been using the land as our own for several years so that ownership will eventually revert to the temple.

Love,
Karl

The initial feelings of abandonment upon arriving at this ashram were unfounded as an adult. Still, they brought back the feelings for me to finally deal with and allow that newly emptied space in my subconscious to be filled with bliss. I closed my eyes and revisited the feelings of abandonment and quietly said to myself, "I am complete with that." The feelings faded away. I still remember the incident, but the feelings of abandonment are gone. If the feelings return in the future, they won't be nearly as intense, and a repetition of the completion statement will allow the remaining feelings to fade away. The stronger the feeling, the more times completions will have to be done. In the end, you are in command of your subconscious.

This ashram/temple is so beautiful yet so empty for me. I find it difficult to form relationships with anybody here. They all prefer to speak in Tamil. Tathananda, the only fluent English speaker, is rarely here. In his absence, a twenty-something button-pushing ashramite named Suvananda is in charge. Tathananda told us that Suvananda spent a year on the Bidadi Ashram restricted to the banyan tree doing puja, and Artis and Swami still could not get through to him. As a last resort, Suvananda was sent to Hyderabad. Which begs the question, was I sent here as a last resort? There is no time for meditation here because we are supposed to be working all the time to restore this temple to its former glory. Pruning rose bushes in bare feet without gloves is my new meditation.

Chapter 23

Incidental

Dear Lynn,

Right now, this Hyderabad temple feels like a minimum-security prison. Eight-foot-high concrete walls surround it with ten rows of electric fence wire another five feet above that. Tathananda is doing the best he can, given the situation. Our rooms are just outside the gates around the temple's side, perched at the top of a small embankment. Tathananda knows we won't run away because there is nowhere to go. I have to eat whatever is prepared, usually rice and samba, when it is ready. There are very few snacks. Only the people who go out on the scooter to do the shopping get snacks because they buy them along with the vegetables and hide them in their rooms. Whenever Tathananda is away, we inmates do the minimum amount of work and hide out during the hottest part of the day. We usually don't get lunch on those days. We eat what is left over from breakfast. The quality of food drops noticeably when Tathananda is away, not that it is great to start with.

Today, a sanyasi came in with a middle-aged man, his father, and his young son. The sanyasi did a lot of Sanskrit chanting, went into the temple, did some more chanting, and then came down to an area with nine small deities and did some more chanting. It all took over an hour. Apparently, this is how the temple operated before handing it over to Swami. Now these sanyasis-for-hire need to ask permission. They will usually be told "No" and our brahmacharis will do the ceremonies.

My Ananda Ghanda (heart) center is growing despite the conditions or more likely because of the conditions here. I feel the blissful glow across my whole chest now, from my waist to my throat. More and more things seem to activate it now.

When Swami said there were 10,000 people at his Jayanti and I could only see 2000, the Indian people I talked to told me it was not a lie, just a little exaggeration. Swami also told us that he is in bliss 10,000 times more than we are. Using the same math as his Jayanti, I think his bliss is more like 2000 times more than we feel, which is still significant but leads me to question the integrity of many of the things I hear. I suspect Swami is one large, blindingly powerful energy center. He once told us that his mental world before enlightenment was 1 acre of ego busyness. Now it is 1000 acres of spiritual bliss. That one acre is still there, but of no concern. I would love to experience 1000 acres of bliss!

When I looked into Tathananda's face intently one day recently while listening to him, I could see his hands in my peripheral vision glowing a bright green. I looked down at his hands, and they were normal. I looked back at his face, and his hands were glowing green again. I don't know what this means. It has only happened a few times.

Today was great; I just read and slept. Today, I also had another spiritual experience. Another small step. Yesterday I was doing the morning Nithya Dhyan meditation routinely enough in the temple, but at the end, during the unclutching part of the meditation, I actually started unclutching (detaching), and the next thing I was aware of was total darkness/blankness. Complete 100% silence without a thought. I took a deep breath and then another, and ever so slowly, thoughts started returning, but not as intensely as before. Hope has been rekindled.

This morning, I started the silent "Who am I" meditation. Every time I noticed a thought come up, I questioned, "Who am I?" and my thoughts would vaporize! Thoughts came up slower and slower. I was almost thought-free.

Tonight, I had my first good conversation with the three ashramite/temple boys. They were amazed that I could sweat while dressing the deity at 5:00 am when they were shivering from the cold. They also expressed amazement that I could carry a 45lb brass deity in one hand and an emergency light in the other when they struggled to hold the brass deity in two hands. We talked about snow and how differently houses are constructed in Canada, and income and expenses in Canada compared with India.

I enjoyed your call today, planning our escape for May. I wish it was tomorrow, but I understand you want to give spirituality every chance to flower after spending all the money you did to get here. At seven months now, I feel like I have already given it my all, and Swami is now incidental to my spiritual quest after the tremendous spiritual awakening he has bestowed on me. I feel what will happen will happen despite Swami, no matter where I am, so I might as well be comfortable in Canada. My intuitive friend back home said I would be in for a big test at the nine-month mark. That is about the time we plan to leave India. I don't know if I should be worried or excited.

I recently had a dream that answered my questioning about why people can't read other people's thoughts. I dreamt I could read people's thoughts as clearly as I could talk to them. Their thoughts often had nothing to do with what they were saying, like someone carrying on a telephone conversation with their friend while talking to you. Their thoughts were not all that interesting, just a bunch of disjointed inner chatter that even the people having the thoughts were not clear about. How disappointing.

Yesterday, we all had a good discussion about food in Canada. They couldn't believe that anybody would have meat with their breakfast (bacon). That night at supper, I just could not stomach eating a cold leftover breakfast of rice and samba. It was the same food we all had cold at lunch. I told them I was not hungry. They couldn't believe I was not hungry. The ashramite in charge ordered take-out jipatis for breakfast. They are deep-fried flatbread. They are incredibly delicious after months of rice and samba and, of course, no supper the night before. They weren't served until 11:00 am, but they were still worth the wait.

One of the temple boys, Haidra, came to my room at 10:30 pm after supper to finish our discussion about spirituality. He told me that shortly after he arrived, he couldn't handle the boredom and asked Tathananda to go back to Bidadi. Tathananda said, "No, working or not working is not the issue. Being here in this different energy is the goal. Just let the energy do its work on you." Haidra says he has learned to be a lot more relaxed and peaceful now. He told me his wife commented that he was much more patient on his last visit home. He says that even his neighbors commented on how much easier it is to talk to him now. Apparently, he had an extremely short fuse and treated his wife like a slave. Haidra says his wife is correct most of the time, and he lets her do what works best. He says that the energy here has helped him a lot. His point was that even though I may not feel spiritually different, like him, others will notice a change when I get home.

Love,
Karl

Haidra could not have been more accurate. When I finally did get back to life in Canada, I quickly became aware of and treasured an unshakable inner core of peace within me that was immune to anything that was happening around me. When I was teaching in my classroom and students were starting to get out of control, my core of peace allowed me the mental space to take a breath and take charge of the situation calmly without anxiety or frustration. I felt I could stay centered and peaceful in just about any situation. I love the new me.

Dear Lynn,

> I dreamed I was an ancient Egyptian walking down a long, wide causeway to a huge pyramid. The causeway was lined on both sides with 30-foot tall stone statues of legendary giants long past that were honored as the creators of all that we enjoy today. I was the involuntary high priest of the pyramid and was leading a procession down the causeway. My status was not exceptional. Anybody with the ability to maintain a meditative state while conducting their daily business could perform my part. Many had the skill. I just happened to be the first one who didn't say no when asked to take on the

responsibility. There just had to be someone to focus energy on for the ceremony to work.

As I walked down the causeway, the priests in the procession focused their energy on me and I, in turn, radiated the energy out around myself in a massive sphere of the most brilliant golden-white light. As the light touched each statue we passed, the solid stone statue raised its right hand into a gesture of greeting so that all 100 or so statues greetings together acknowledged the level of the collective energy of the procession. The acknowledgment of the statues allowed a huge doorway on the side of the pyramid to become visible. As the massive ball of golden white light got closer to the pyramid, the stone door in the pyramid's side opened. The door was big enough for the giants depicted by the statues to walk through proudly. Inside the pyramid, our energy would recharge and refocus the pyramid. The ceremony I was performing was freely taught to all the people of the land, so all could contribute their energy when needed, but only one person could be the focal point of the collective energy—one that could maintain a detached meditative state while walking to keep the ball of light brilliant and powerful enough to affect the statues on both sides of the causeway at once. I felt honored and trapped at the same time. I appreciated the honor bestowed on me to be the focal point that manipulates the energies to do what is necessary, but simultaneously, I had to give up everything in my life to keep my energy pure, detached, and undistractable.

In spite of everybody being taught as much of the process as they chose to participate in, very few had the desire and skill even to attempt the reclusive training to replace me eventually. The public training was necessary to find enough people to provide the purest energy. Sadly, fewer and fewer people were able to remain focused long enough to create the clear intentioned energy and to avoid becoming distracted with their lives and cloud the energy. The clouding of the participant's energies was taking a toll on my ability to remain detached. Very soon, I would not be able to continue with my work, and there was no one interested in replacing me. The pyramid would become just another mysterious monument from the past. Nobody would remember how to unlock its alchemical secrets to keep the world energetically balanced.

The dream made me feel sad that so much knowledge and wisdom was being lost, but at the same time, I accepted that it was a natural consequence of the way the world was devolving. These same feelings of missed opportunity and wisdom that should have been passed on to the next generation, which is now lost to history, happen when I enter any place of worship.

Tathananda returned this morning. After breakfast, he started a little heart to heart, asking what my and your intentions were before coming to India. Then we talked about the jobs I did in Bidadi ashram, and he tried to reprimand me for not being more organized in what I was working on in Bidadi. I explained that I tried for quite a while to be organized before I finally accepted the way things were. Then we talked about how much influence the young people have and why things aren't running more smoothly at Bidadi. Tathananda said we would talk more. We never did.

When I meditate now, it is easier to get to the point of no thoughts. Is the next step to astral travel to realize I am more than the body?

Tonight at supper, Tejananda realized that in forty-four days, his Ananda Yogum training is over. His dad will come and take him back to the family farm, so he wanted me to wake him at 3:00 am for his remaining forty-four days so he could do all his meditations and still get the deities dressed before the power turned off at 6:00 am. Not going to happen!

Our kitchen kid, Nareshananda, asked for my help to clean the kitchen and do the dishes tonight. I was happy to help where I could. I took one look at the disaster and knew this was beyond catching up on a few days of neglect. This was going to take a lot of patient training in a language I didn't understand. Just imagine a seventeen-year-old who has never cooked outside of his mother's kitchen now in charge

> of a kitchen cooking for six adults and twenty village kids. Pots, pans, and dishes were piled up on the curb out front because he couldn't be bothered to bring them into the kitchen and put them away. The only time he did any dishes was when he needed a pot to cook in. The kitchen itself is unbelievably filthy. There was food swept into corners. Splatters of food everywhere and more flies than a garbage dump. The floor looked like you needed to put on a Hazmat suit before you could get within ten feet of the place. I can't believe we are all still alive!

Love,
Karl

Seven days into my Hyderabad stay and connecting with Lynn in Bidadi is still more miss than hit. The only phone line is in the temple where the public views the deities, so the phone is only plugged in when the public is least likely to show up, usually for a few hours in the middle of the day. However, the phone in Bidadi was equally difficult to access because of long lines of people wanting the use the only phone in the office there. The internet was the preferred method of contact. I copied out my handwritten message for Lynn on the computer and arranged for a trip to Shamshabad to use the internet.

Dear Lynn,

It was Haidraananda's birthday, so I wanted to take him into Shamshabad and get him something special to eat. Suvananda told Haidra he had to finish his laundry first, then he had to take a bath. Finally, with chores completed, he asked Suvananda again if he could go with me. Suva said, "No!" As if that were not enough, he went on to tell Haidraananda that if he went anyway, he would tell Swami, and he would never be allowed to take a blessing from Swami for the rest of his life. He would be banned from all Dhyanapeetam ashrams forever. Making decisions about how Swami will punish or bless anybody is way beyond Suvananda's job description. I was furious when I heard this (button pushed!). Not only was Haidraananda not allowed to leave the temple on his birthday, but he got blackmailed as a gift from Suvananda. Suvananda then told me he would take me to Shamshabad on the scooter to use the internet. I just about punched him in the nose right there. I asked him why he should be the one to drive me when Haidraananda was just as capable. Suvananda gave us his standard response, "No! It's not like that! Only if an ashramite has business they can go." I told him he better go and take care of his business then. I took an auto-rickshaw by myself to remove the temptation to do something I might later regret. By the time I found an internet cafe and waited for my turn, my email finally got sent near five. I sure hope Tathananda has the correct user ID and password to connect to the internet at the temple tomorrow! I picked up a container of two hundred eclairs, chocolate-filled toffee candies, for Haidrananda's birthday. When I got back to the temple, Haidraananda and I went to my room to talk. He ate just about all the eclairs.

The next morning, Tathananda was back before breakfast. Suvananda rushed out to meet him. Haidraananda and I happened to be just on the other side of the temple wall from Suvananda, where we could clearly hear Suva telling Tathananda all about our little confrontation the day before. I'm sure Suvananda was expecting Tathananda to chastise Haidrananda all over again. Instead, Tathananda reprimanded Suvananda for quite a long time. We couldn't understand much because it was in Telugu, but it was clear that Suvananda was getting a good firing. Tathananda was his grouchy self at breakfast, complaining about everything from the food's temperature to the samba's consistency. I tried to change the subject of the conversation by commenting on how there were a lot of tears when Swami left the Bidadi Ashram for his trip. Tathananda was surprised I knew what was happening in Bidadi. I told him I talked to Lynn on the phone, to which he responded that he was instructed that I should not be allowed phone access to call any woman, including my wife. He asked Haidraananda how his back was doing, and Haidraananda told him it is slowly getting better and the exercise and tablets the doctor gave him are helping. Tathananda angrily told Haidraananda to throw away the pills, let the body heal itself, and use the pain to learn how to hold the body in the correct position, so there isn't pain naturally.

Tathananda also told Haidraananda that he needed to get up early in the morning's soft light when the sun is just rising to make his day beautiful. Waiting until the sun is already up makes one antagonistic all day long. And the cold Haidrananda feels from sleeping on the concrete floor is a healing cold. It is beautiful! I am no doctor, but cold concrete brings thoughts of pain and arthritis, and anybody that has to get up before the sun just gets tired. Tathananda was not a doctor any more than I was.

Later on, during breakfast, Tathananda asked Haidrananda to go into Hyderabad and get the English books to teach his English student. Then he told Haidrananda to take me along. Suvananda was looking a little like a whipped dog. Tathananda ended up driving us into Hyderabad on his way to take care of his own business. Haidrananda and I enjoyed a pizza lunch for his belated birthday. To help Haidrananda understand the West a little more, he tried to guess what the pizza bill should be. He guessed 80rs. When I told him it was 750rs, he couldn't believe it. It was the first time he ever had pizza. Judging by his reaction to the price, it was probably his last. From there, we went to a coffee shop where we had strawberry frappes. It was heavenly coming from an ashram with no refrigeration. Once again, Haidrananda guessed about 10% of the bill. Haidrananada had a good birthday.

Tathananda asked me how our trip to Hyderabad went yesterday. I told him about the pizza lunch. His smile told me he approved. When I told him about my attempt to renew my visa, he asked me how much it would cost. I told him I didn't know. He overreacted and told me I was completely wrong. The travel agent is going to gouge me now. Tathananda said I should have known ahead of time how much it would cost. I asked him how I could have done that without internet or the ability to speak Telegu? All he could say was how wrong I was, but not what I could have done differently. I called different travel agents until I could make myself understood. The English-speaking agent gave me a website address to renew my visa myself with a credit card. Conversations with Tathananda are getting a little too bipolar for my comfort.

Today, I copied all the Telugu Quantum Memory Program files off Tathananda's laptop so Haidrananda and I can transcribe the information to create an English version. I could also use the information to help my students back in Canada. I have many mental images about how the finished book will look, complete with sketches to show hand positions. I hope Mom can help with the sketching. I get a strong feeling that this is one of the reasons I am here at this time to bring this information to the West.

Today is the first day I can use the internet in the Hyderabad Temple. I am typing virtually nonstop, not knowing how long this access will be available. Tathananda is in America giving workshops, so it is less likely that he will interrupt things. Govindananda will be leaving in a few days to give his workshops, so he is preoccupied, but I still have chaos theory to contend with!!

While meditating this morning, I randomly wondered if chickadees in India could communicate with chickadees in Canada. Since animals communicate telepathically, they probably can. Today I went into Hyderabad with Haidrananda for his back physiotherapy. I told him that is what he gets for sleeping on a mat on concrete! He says he wrenched his back while carrying a 50lb propane cylinder on the back of a scooter when the driver went through a big pothole. It really hurt then and has continued to hurt ever since.

After Haidrananda's physiotherapy, we went to an internet shop to get my visa application completed. The tiny shop had a dozen computers with wires and power bars everywhere. Only half of them worked. I was about halfway through the transaction. My charge card number was entered, my passport information was all entered, and then the owner wanted to use the computer. I couldn't believe it! He said, "Just one minute," but I know what an Indian minute can mean. Since I needed his cooperation to get the printing done, I relented. He thanked me and spent the next 15 minutes filling out some form and printing it for another customer. When I finally got back on the computer, the visa process went more smoothly than the chaos of this room suggested. We were out of there in about 10 minutes and only 15rs poorer. I'm sure the price was reduced due to my frustration with the shop owner's interruption.

From the internet shop, we went back to the pizza place for lunch. The lunch turned into a lesson in using cutlery for Haidrananda, who told me he had never used a knife or fork before. After pizza, we went to Coffee World across the street for a caramel frappe. You would have loved being in Coffee World, Lynn. It was a Canadian store except for what you could see out the windows.

After our pizza and frappe, the day was only half over. Haidrananda suggested we do some tourist-type thing. We decided to see this massive Muslim-styled arch in the middle of Hyderabad called the Charminar. Think Arc de Triumph. Charminar is over 200 feet high with tight little spiral staircases in all four corners. The ornate carvings and architecture were awe-inspiring. Admission was 5rs for Indians, 100rs for foreigners! The view was amazing from the top. The railings were only 2 feet high—a testament to the height of the people who built the thing. Half a block away was a huge mosque. The sign out front of the mosque claims it is the second biggest in the world. A guide came up to us and started talking. I told him to go away a few times. I guess I wasn't assertive enough. At the end of his 5-minute description of some decorated rocks that he said were tombs of past kings, he wanted 50rs. I gave him 20rs and ignored all his Tamil gibberish, which Haidrananda said was his insults about cheap foreigners!

From the mosque, we went to Fort Golconda. It is similar to the palace on the rock in Sigiriya in Sri Lanka. There are easily over 1000 stairs carved into the rock to get up to the big administration buildings at the top. I should have counted the steps so I could compare! According to the brochure, there is also a mosque and giant water tank on the hill filled with water from an aquifer five miles long. We told the guide we didn't want his help. He got quite indignant and was swearing at us in Telegu, according to Haidrananda. Haidrananda told the guy taking tickets, and the ticket taker came out and yelled something at the guy who looked a little sheepish now and left us alone. The big buildings at the top of the rock had a massive stone wall built up around it one and a half miles in circumference. The townsite for all the military, government officials, and support staff was surrounded by another wall 80 feet high in many places. The wall is five miles in circumference with an extensive moat around the outside. I am amazed at how much work, blood, sweat, and tears it took to build everything to protect what we later learned was a thriving diamond trade. There was yet another wall that encompassed three small villages just outside the second wall. The last wall looked like it encompassed hundreds of square miles. The massive gates looked like they haven't operated in a century or three, but they are still hanging in the open position on their original hinges. They look like they are 60 feet high, opening to a sharp 90-degree right turn in the road followed by another 90-degree left turn that slowed traffic to a crawl as it negotiated its way through the turns.

We had to wait in the bus loop at Fort Golconaa for our bus home, a dusty gravel open area surrounded by street vendors, dogs, and four cows, for about 20 minutes. The quality of the watermelon is dropping. Must be getting to the end of the two-month growing season or getting end-of-the-day leftovers. Grapes are being sold all over the place right now. There are carts and carts of them everywhere you go. Grapes are not recommended for tourists without washing, but then the washing water is an issue itself. Another popular drink is cane juice. The vendors have a machine that looks like the top part of a wringer washing machine. They stick the cane in, and the rollers crush the cane and squeeze the juice out. They fold the squished cane in half and run it through again, then fold and squish 4 or 5 times again. The juice tastes great, but I make sure a few people have gone before me to rinse out all the fly poop, so the juice I get is cleaner than if I was the first one.

When the bus finally came, the conductor was the same young woman that we rode with before. She was asking Haidrananda questions about me last time. This time she asked Haidrananda, "Does he remember me?" After Haidrananda gave me the translation, I pointed to her ticket box with the big dent in the side and mimicked the motion of her hitting the grab bar on the bus ceiling with it. She gave me a big smile because she is the only one who signals the driver that way as far as I know. So she knew I remembered. She then told Haidrananda exactly which bus to connect with and how to find it. During the bus trip, a woman brought what looked like a 14-year-old blind boy on the bus. He appeared to be handicapped as well. After a short time, he started singing and keeping time by slapping his thighs. He was excellent. Quite a few of the passengers stopped talking and watched him. One passenger spoke to the boy in Telugu, and the boy sang a different song. The passenger paid the boy for his song. After about a 45-minute trip, the friendly conductor came over and tapped Haidrananda on the shoulder and told him it was time to get off. She pointed out the window to the bus that would take us to the village of Satamarai. I gave her an Anjali Mudra as a thank you by placing my hands together, palms touching with fingers pointing up, closing my eyes, and bowing slightly. She responded with a big smile as we disembarked. When I looked back, she was still watching us, one more Anjali Mudra and another big smile as her bus pulled away. The bus she pointed out dropped us as planned at Satamarai.

I bought another kilogram of eclairs while Haidrananda phoned his wife from the telephone booth. We walked the two kilometers back to the temple in the dark. As we walked through the small village closest to the temple, some young revelers were getting carried away with colored powders. It was a celebration called Holi, where revelers throw water on each other colored with fluorescent powders. This group of people was going door to door—well, it was more like curtain to curtain since there really weren't any doors! They would just run into a house, cover the occupants with color, and run out to the next place. We timed our walk to avoid them by passing when they just ran into a house. Apparently, they were out one night too early. We got back to the temple at 9:00 pm. I think I will hide out in my room tomorrow until the colors pass. Haidrananda assured me nobody would dare color a temple. It would be bad karma for lifetimes to come. The young revelers who couldn't get the day right didn't get the temple memo either and colored the temple anyway.

Love,

Karl

Chapter 24

Drama with Detachment

Dear Lynn,

Govindananda asked how our trip went yesterday in Hyderabad at breakfast. I briefly told him about the three tourist sites we visited. After I finished, he told me how irresponsible Haidrananda was. He should have been handing out flyers yesterday afternoon for the women's clinic at the temple. Haidrananda was worried about it yesterday, but I convinced him that someone would take over if he wasn't there. Sure enough, Suvananda had to do it. Suvananda, however, hired a pickup truck backed auto-rickshaw and sat in the back with loudspeakers talking about the clinic while six kids ran around handing out the flyers. I told Govindananda it was my idea that

Haidrananda did not return for flyer duty, but he kept talking like I hadn’t said anything. I didn't interrupt anymore to let him finish talking and left the table. After lunch, Govindananda went into Shamshabad to speak to a group of yoga students about meditation. Apparently, he gave them an introduction yesterday, but today they wanted more.

That afternoon while I was reading in my room, a big group of kids came screaming up to the temple and colored all the brahmacharis who didn't take cover in time. Now two brahmacharis are walking around looking like blue Smurfs. The walls and doors of their rooms are also all colored. They didn't quite close the door in time. I closed my shutters and locked my door when I heard them coming and continued reading. After they left, the deadbolt on the outside of my door was slid into the locked position. I just continued to read and the first person to walk by opened it for me.

We did Arati early at 5:00 pm today because there is an especially auspicious eclipse of the moon tonight. The villagers here are very superstitious about having to be outside, or all your food gets spoiled. You have to clean your house before the eclipse and again after. These eclipse rituals were in addition to the ordinarily exuberant color-throwing Holi celebrations. No wonder the kids were so excited. The next morning, we were not allowed into the temple until after 7:30 am when the official eclipse was over.

Govindananda was rushing us all around, making last-minute preparations for the gynecological medical clinic today. The volunteer doctors saw 150 village patients between 8:30 am and noon. I talked with the gynecologist husband, who told me they like to give back to the community that has given them so much. They try to do free medical camps like this once a week. His wife got things rolling about two and a half years ago. Since then, the gynecological society sets them up for the doctors, so all members contribute their free time equitably.

That evening, I arrived at the sanctum sanctorum to hear one of the brahmacharis complaining about how I carry the Mayroo and small brass deity from the Ananda Saba downstairs to the temple upstairs. The Mayroo is about 50lbs, so I carry it under one arm resting on my left hip; the multi-handed Shiva deity I hold like a bucket by the brass ring around the top. It was alleged that I didn't show enough respect (some things don't need a translator). It was decided the complaining brahmachari could carry the brass deities himself with all the respect he wanted to give them.

Our watchman was telling Tejananda and me that he is leaving soon. Tejananda speaks only Tamil, the watchman only Hindi, and then there is me! We managed to communicate that he earns 2200rs per month here. When he leaves and goes back to Nepal, he will make 3500rs a month, and it is way too hot here compared to Nepal.

Supper was taking longer than usual, and Govindananda was pacing back and forth. I went over to the temple's mini-deity corner, turned off the light, and watched the moon. I felt a deep peace welling up inside me, slowly expanding until it filled every space in my being. Tears filled my eyes. I felt like I was a brilliant light shining out across the cosmos. I just stared at the moon in bliss with no thoughts until, of course, I thought about how wonderful it felt to have no thoughts. The peace within ebbed and flowed; thoughts came and went. Was this the moment I had come to India for?

The more I meditate, the easier it is to find those moments of peace. The intensity and duration of the peace changes, but it is always there. I have discovered the better I honor my body with good food, exercise, and reduced caffeine, the stronger the feelings.

The next day was pretty quiet until I confronted Suvananda that evening about the new Arati wicks he was to buy a couple of weeks ago. His position as a financial controller is a mystery to us that only a Swami could understand. A part of me is frustrated with his incompetence, and another part of me is in peace, accepting that some of our duties cannot be carried out, and that is just life. He had many excuses and blaming about why there were no Arati wicks, which didn't do anything to absolve him of his responsibility. We were all learning; wicks were incidental. Without wicks, I couldn't perform the Arati, so I told Suvananda he could perform the Arati. He said something rude in Tamil to Nareshananda, which caused him to leave the room angrily. I found out later that Suvananda passed the buck and told Naresh to do the preparations. And just to make himself feel a little better, he gave Haidranandaa a firing for not asking permission to translate the QMP discourses. Permission is hardly necessary when the person you need to ask permission of is the one you are working with doing the task.

Tathananda phoned today to check up on us. He asked questions of each of us. Suvananda told Tathananda how Nareshananda lost 10kg from his already too slim frame. Tathananda fired them for using the scale in the ashram. He said it was unreliable, and they were idiots for using it. He used the word idiot quite a few times. This scale was the same one Tathananda told Suva to use to weigh packages for shipping—packages that are so heavy, they both stand on the scale so I can hand them the package to calculate the difference. Sometimes it is easier to accept how it has always been done than to try to convince people there is an easier alternative. It sounds like how you weigh someone is more important than their health, or is it the Indian way of expressing closeness by firing?

Another day and the pump in the water well is still not working. We have a large enough reservoir on the roof, so we won't run short for a few days yet. On my walk to the village that evening with Haidranandaa, we talked about Suvananda and his attitude. I tried to help him understand that Suva doesn't try to be mean or difficult intentionally. Some people work well with others; some people don't. I know these things intellectually, but when the realization hits me in the heart center, I feel like I have awakened to a deeper level of understanding. During Nithya Dhyan meditation this morning, I came to this understanding when I briefly opened my eyes during the chaotic breathing part because something sounded off. I saw that Suva was sitting peacefully, not chaotic breathing at all.

My first thought was to tell him to do the meditation properly, but any verbal exchange would disrupt my peaceful mood more than opening my eyes already had. I closed my eyes again and realized that not only would it mess up my space, but he wouldn't comply anyway, which made me further realize that by not doing the chaotic breathing part, he would not gain any benefit from the rest of the meditation. I wondered if he realized the consequences of his inaction. Then I felt my heart center warm, and I understood that he doesn't choose to be the way he is. The synchronicity of us both being here in this moment is something for both of us to grow from. I want to learn everything I can from this obstacle to my enlightenment, so I don't have to deal with his likes again. I won't be bothered by people like him anymore or attract his likes into my life because I have resolved that Samskara/Engram. I saw the whole setup in a flash during my meditation. Now I have to allow Suva to be and detach from the drama he creates without getting caught up in it. When you find peace with something that normally triggers you, the situations that once triggered you don't stop happening. You stop being triggered by them, and life becomes a little more blissful.

Govindananda tried talking to Suvananda at supper. Suva turned everything into an opportunity to brag about himself. At one point, Suva was talking about Haidranandaa taking off to the doctor, and he should have made vegetables before he went because it only takes a minute to cut up vegetables. Govindananda then asked Suva why he didn't do it if he knew it needed doing. Suva gave his typical response, "No! It's not like that!" It only takes a minute. It's very easy. Govindananda just stopped talking to him!

Love,

Karl

Dear Lynn,

The sun had to rise four diameters above the horizon this morning before the pollution thinned out enough to let the sun shine a dull red. It immediately disappeared again and wasn't visible until ten diameters, when streaks of light from the sun appeared in the sky like car headlights shining through the trees. It made for a beautifully choreographed play of shadows on the clouds before the sun finally rose for the day. I was concerned about what was in the air to make it so impenetrable to the sun.

Meditation was beautiful this morning. I fell into myself. As I fell, I realized I wasn't falling; I was shrinking. I shrunk to a couple of sizes smaller than my body. My consciousness was floating effortlessly around inside my physical form. Tears streamed down my cheeks as I let my thoughts aimlessly drift by in a completely detached way, like walking through a crowd of people enjoying the closeness and familiarity without getting wrapped up in judgment about who looked more successful, taller, angrier, or any of our petty little differences. The rest of the day was blissfully dreamlike. I never really came 100% back to earth. Suva wasn't even around most of the day!

At lunch, Govindananda was telling us about plans for Telegu New Year. Govindananda told us it is customary for people to hire a crier to recite all the important events for the coming year. Suva started telling us all the list of things the crier would be announcing for the temple. Govindananda looked at him in shock and asked him where he got his information from. Suva reflexively expressed his usual deflection, "No, it's not like that!" Govindananda interrupted him and told him it was not his place to make those kinds of decisions. More deflections and pronouncements that made it clear Suva was not listening. Govindananda realized he was falling into the trap of trying to convince Suva of anything and told him to shut up! This was another example of how Suva can passionately express his point of view in spite of irrefutable evidence to the contrary.

Govindananda was telling me how one of the centers he helped get organized was self-sufficient because the people who lived there paid rent and supported it. Another center was growing quickly. They are currently looking for a temple like this to be donated to make a big step up. Govindananda told me he would take a couple of the brahmacharis from here to do the day-to-day routines. The future of me as a brahmachari is getting clearer. My Western school teacher's mind wants to be an enlightened master before allowing myself to even think about helping anybody else find their path to enlightenment. The picture being painted for me by Govindananada is one of service and the possibility of enlightenment coming in the act of being of service.

Govindananda came to breakfast full of frustration, telling us to leave our stupid minds outside the temple and not compare anything. We need to leave our stupid judgments and angry behaviors outside. They are just making us angry. He went on and on about it, kind of like Suva does when he gets an idea he feels compelled to share. It was so hard to sit there and detach. My feelings were showing me a subconscious issue that needed to see the light of day. A trip into Hyderabad would be nice today. I have to ask permission of Baktananda, five years my junior, to go into Hyderabad. Since he is not on the continent, approval means email. I grudgingly sent it. There is that button being pushed again. How can I blissfully float through life enlightened with all these subconscious issues popping up?

The more I work with Haidrananda trying to translate Tamil for this book, the more I understand the Tamil language. The language sounds confusing and convoluted. A single English sentence can take five minutes in Tamil and numerous repetitions of the same information in slightly different ways to express. Sometimes the Tamil speaker explains his concept so many different times that he can't remember what he said the first time, and the information changes. It was challenging to find the point the speaker in the recording was trying to get across so I could connect the ideas into a nicely flowing book. Translating Tamil into English with Haidrananda was much more work than I thought it would be.

I got a little carried away with the camphor on the multi-tiered Arati lamp today. When I passed the lit lamp to Nareshananda, the flames were three feet high. The heat was powerful, and the look on his face was priceless. Naresh didn't know whether to laugh or scream. He gingerly took the lamp and tried one wave back and forth, but the heat was too intense. He passed it back to me with his arm fully extended while his other hand shielded his face from the heat. I handed him the next Arati lamp so he could continue his Arati while I took the blazing Arati lamp out of the sanctum santorum for the always-present village kids to take care of. They threw sand on it and put it out pretty fast, but it took four hours of me scrubbing to clean off the glazed-on soot.

I have been teaching English class to the village kids in the temple for a couple of weeks. I am still resistant to it. The class is conversational in English. I read them a newspaper article in an English paper and then ask them questions about the article. The interpreter explains, and the students write their answers in their notebooks. I have trouble coming up with a list of twenty questions about the article before the class, but I don't seem to have any problem during the class with all the students in front of me. I need to have more faith in myself and trust it will flow when I need it. Maybe that is how Swami was hoping we could recite his book.

The police came today about a robbery at the temple that happened four months ago. They found a lot of the temple stuff with other plunder. The police brought the guy to the temple in leg irons and had him explain his side of the story. I didn't understand Tamil, and Haidranandaa, who interpreted for me later, said he didn't get it all, but there was something about if the doors weren't properly locked, he can't be charged. The discussion took a couple of hours. In the end, Suvananda had to go in the police car to the police station and fill out another "invitation," as they had lost the original. A lot of the village homes only have a curtain for a front door. Does the properly-locked-door loophole mean village homes are open to thievery?

Govindananda knows Tamil well enough that 90% of the table talk at mealtimes is in Tamil. I only get English when it is an official announcement now. I'm sure I could ask them to speak English more, but that would kill the spontaneity of their joking and conversation and leave out a couple of the temple boys who don't understand English at all. I don't need to understand Tamil to water the plants or to do the dishes. Mindless menial jobs are perfect for questioning my decisions. Successful in attaining enlightenment or not, I will never be the same as when I came to India.

Haidrananda and I are getting close to finishing the translation of QMP. It was a pretty quiet and productive day until Nareshananda came into the computer room. He was quiet, but he kept farting. The smell was putrid. We had to leave the room each time he broke wind. He must have been farting laughing gas because every time he let one go, he couldn't stop laughing. He would fall down on the floor and roll around laughing. It was kind of fun, but it sure slowed down the translation. Now I know how temple brats entertain themselves: a little cabbage for lunch, and soon there is entertainment for all.

At lunchtime, Haidrananda and I went to make preparations. I am the dishwasher, outside on the little stool under the tap. I told them I couldn't cook with all the products labeled in Telugu plus not knowing how to prepare some of the Indian ingredients. I had no idea how to deal with drumsticks. I just stay out of the kitchen! I digress. When I threw open the kitchen door, there was Naresh halfway through a big papaya. Papayas fresh off the tree are halfway between a cantaloupe and a watermelon in size. They are heavenly to eat. To me, they taste more like an apricot. We gave him a good firing and kicked him out of the kitchen. I cut up what was left and went and got our gardener to share it with. When the gardener finally arrived, the first thing he did was plop both of his filthy hard-working hands on top of the freshly cut fruit and start chanting a mantra to bless the fruit. Next time he can pick his own fruit. We ate the fruit anyway!

Love,

Karl

Chapter 25

Canadian Culture

Dear Lynn,

Today, we witnessed the other side of Govindananda. He was casually asking Suvananda how Tejananda's stomach was doing these days, expecting to hear a story of how the situation was resolved. Suvananda shared that Tejananda still had a stomach ache fifteen days later. Suvananda went on to tell Govindananda that on Teja's last check-up, he also had low blood pressure because he ran for about ten minutes to get to the hospital. Govindananda was shocked by Suvananda's diagnostics! Govindananda gave him a big, long firing for making a medical diagnosis with no qualifications on top of the fact that any idiot knows you don't get low blood pressure from running.

Govindananda asked him if everybody who runs has low blood pressure then. Suvananda gave his typical response, "No, It's not like that." Govindananda fired him all over again. Govindananda then ironically gave everybody a firing because we all yelled at Suvananda. Govindananda told us that Suvananda had accepted responsibility for the whole ashram. Unless anybody here was willing to accept that responsibility, he had better keep his stupid comments to himself. It was hard not to laugh at the irony of the situation. He gave us a firing for doing precisely what he had just done! The scary part for me was nobody else made the connection. I explained the irony to the guys the next day in my English class, and we all had a good laugh once the interpreter explained it. Tathananda gave everybody the same firing all over again shortly after Govidananda. Is there some sort of firing quota I'm not privy to?

Every night, Tejananda and Haidrananda walk the dozen or so village kids home in the dark after their supper at the temple. The kids are quite capable of getting home on their own, but Tejananda has a girlfriend back home, and he uses the walk as an excuse to call her from the much more reliable village phone booth every night. Unfortunately, Tejananda wasn't feeling well enough tonight, so I went with Haidrananda. When the watchman saw us from his seat on the sidewalk out front of his converted garden shed, he joined us, and the three of us walked the village kids home. Haidra and the watchman are about the same age. With Haidrananda's translating, we managed a conversation. The conversation started with our watchman saying something to Haidrananda that made him laugh for quite a while. Finally, I got the translation: he was so happy to be walking away from the prison! Haidrananda and I had been talking carefully about how the temple felt like a prison earlier. Our exclusive temple prison club just got its third member. We all shared our frustrations about the place. It was a good temple brat bonding time! There is something about this place that makes it feel like Hotel California: you can check out any time you like, but you can never leave. I keep expecting to find some secret room where the old brahmacharis go to die.

I started teaching the guys how to use the computer yesterday. I downloaded a free typing program, and now they are all fighting over who gets to use the computer. I am still amazed that Haidrananda is thirty-something with an engineering degree, and he doesn't know how to use a computer. I showed him how to navigate YouTube after lunch, and I couldn't get him off all afternoon. Apparently, this is the first time he has seen videos besides TV. I hope YouTube addiction doesn't incur karma!

This morning, Nareshananda finally got his medicine for constipation and took his first 5ml dose right away. He doesn't speak English, but he kept saying, "This is honey!" as he took sip after sip. Before lunch, the whole 60ml bottle was empty. His biggest mistake was going to ask Suvananda for another bottle. Since it was a prescription, Suvananda had to ask Govindananda; he asked at the lunch table. Ooooh, Govindananda let Nareshananda have it. He called Naresh a stupid donkey who had done an idiotic thing for even an immature child to do. He went on and on. In the end, he told

Suva not to buy any medicine for any of us, and trips to visit the doctor were officially not allowed anymore. If anybody gets sick, they can go to their rooms and die. At least there, they will rot without smelling up the rest of the place. Govindananda was in fine form by the end of that firing.

Naresh was pooping and farting all afternoon. He would let out a huge uncontrollable fart, and then get this concerned look on his face and run off to the bathroom. We were all rolling on the ground, laughing. Constipation cured!

We got a call from one of our brahmachari's parents today just after his eighteenth birthday on the temple phone. His parents wanted to end his brahmacharya days so he could go home to take advantage of the government grant for engineering school to support his family. Tejananda wants to get the degree, but he also wants brahmacharya. He wanted some advice from his friends. A few days later, his father came and took him back to the family village.

This morning, I was dreaming that I was walking along a dirt road in the woods with my military squad. We were looking out for the enemy with all the trucks and guns that make the army what it is when all of a sudden, the guy standing up in the back of a jeep holding a big machine gun at the front of our procession slowly turned around and pointed the gun directly at me. I rolled out of formation down on the ground and over behind a truck. The machine gunner slowly and methodically shot a very neat line of holes along the side of the truck with amazing precision. I knew I had to get away from the truck before it blew up. Just then, I heard a plop on the pillow beside my head. I was thinking cockroach. I quickly made a sweeping motion with the back of my hand. I hit something cockroach size. I heard it hit the bedpost. My adrenaline was pumping and the light was on. I searched but couldn't find anything anywhere. I pulled back the sheet, shook it out, and removed the pillow, but still nothing. I swept the entire room with the broom, yet nothing. It was 5:30 am. I was tired and seriously thought that after all that searching, it was probably safe to get back into bed when I noticed a four-inch-long scorpion crawling up the wall at the head of my bed. I just stood there wondering how I could have brushed that away with my hand without getting stung. I smacked it on the wall with the broom, but it fell behind the bed. With a trusty flashlight and the broom, I found it and tried to sweep the body out, but it was still alive and coming full speed for me. They sure move fast, but not as quickly as my broom. I swept the now dead body into the opposite corner of the room to show my friends later. Good thing this all happened before 6:00 am when the power goes off for four hours, and it would be dark! I wondered if the scorpion has any friends or family wandering around the other corners of my room. My adrenaline was still pumping. Thank you, spirit, for a prophetic dream to get me pumped for action.

During my English class, I asked if any of the guys had been stung by a scorpion. All but one had. Apparently, it hurts intensely for a couple of hours, but there is no lasting damage. I was happy I didn't have to find out first hand.

This evening, Haidrananda confided in me that he took Suva's cell phone from where he had left it on the table at lunch. We all made comments to Suva at lunch to remember his phone. Apparently, Haidrananda came back an hour or so later, and it was still there. He picked it up and hid it. About four weeks ago, I used a plate that I had seen Suva using from time to time. I did not do it to upset anybody, but because everybody just grabs what is there. He came over to talk to me like I was a little kid. "You saw me using this plate. Why are you using my plate?" He sounded like he was going to cry, so I gave him his precious plate and didn't use it again. However, I did hide it in the kitchen a few days later on a shelf a little higher than his eye level and put a bag of beans on it so you could only see the edge of the entire plate. I showed the other guys; they all laughed and thought it was great. A week later, Suva cleaned out the whole kitchen until 1:30 am and still did not find his plate. The guys are positive that for him to miss the plate in so conspicuous a place, Swami must be in on the game. It works for me!!

Suva held a meeting today after supper. He was sure one of the village kids must have taken his phone. Not only was he sure it was a village kid, he thought he knew which kid it was and wanted Haidrananda to take him to the kid's house in the village to get his phone back from the little thief. It was just like Suva to accuse the nicest kid. This kid comes early every day so he can do all the dishes before supper. There is a big pile of dishes with all the cooking pots from breakfast, lunch, and dinner. Haidrananda had hidden the phone on some newspapers on top of the fridge in the kitchen. The fridge is used as a cupboard because it hasn't worked for a long time. Someone quietly commented about how the day's paper was on the fridge, and nobody had read it yet. Suva rushed to get the paper because he always has to read the paper first. Voila! He found his cell phone. He swore the dishwashing kid hid it there so he could pick it up the next day.

When we started walking the village kids home at about 9:00 pm, a couple of the kids showed me how they could put their finger in their mouth and make a pop sound by twisting their finger out sideways. I showed them how I could press my tongue to the inside of my upper lip and then force my tongue out with air pressure to make the same sound, but many more pops much faster. They hooted with laughter and chattered away in Telugu and then kept bugging me to do it again and again. One of the boys trying to mimic me got pretty close to getting it. Then I whistled a little bit. They laughed all over again. I was amazed that none of them knew how to whistle. They were busy trying to copy me for quite a while. When we got to the phone booth, I bought some drinks. They were miniature Coke bottles that only cost 7rs. The best part was now I had bottle caps. I showed the kids how to send the bottle caps flying like miniature frisbees by using your fingers' snapping action to propel them. They loved it. I had a half dozen kids in this class! By the time we walked back through the village, one of the boys was doing pretty well. All he needs now is a pocket full of bottle caps. Nothing like spreading a little Canadian culture!

Today, Haidrananda and I went into Hyderabad while handing out Ugadi (Telugu New Year) pamphlets. We had a nice pizza lunch and a lichi frappe with a cup of cane juice on the way home. Walking back to the temple, Suva went speeding by on the scooter. He keeps giving Haidrananda a bad time about just about anything his twisted little mind can come up with. When Haidrananda, Tejananda, and I were walking the kids home tonight, we had a good heart to heart about how to handle Suva. Haidrananda was just quietly taking Suva's abuse. We told Haidrananda not to take Suva's abuse but to return the abuse and point out a few of the things Suva should not be doing in return. Suva provides lots of examples of how to break his own rules. Haidrananda was feeling much less frustrated.

Fires are burning again tonight on the horizon. A few kilometers away, we can see massive kilometer-wide fires burning. When the wind is blowing towards us, most of the time, there is no doubt that the fire is in the garbage dump. The smoke and smell are disgusting. No wonder they wait till dark. The next morning, the smoke is thick, and the sun takes a long time to rise above the haze.

Suva confronted me about where I was yesterday. I told him I went to Shamshabad to get a bug screen for my window. I did get a bug screen but in Hyderabad. He told me I was lying. He said I was with Haidrananda. I told him just because he saw the two of us walking together doesn't mean we spent the whole day together. And what if we did? What is wrong with that? Suva was shaking. He was so mad, but he couldn't think of anything else to say and walked away. After our little tete-a-tete, I realized I wasn't upset with Suva. It was the fact that I had to ask permission to go to town to replace the bug screen on my window. I am having trouble keeping my buttons from being pushed. Australia wouldn't be the same from a travel brochure in an Indian jail cell. I will have to accept I still have buttons to push and blissfully work on detaching.

Today, Haidrananda and I went into Shamshabad to deliver more Ugadi flyers after my English class. Govindananda just returned to the temple today after opening a new center in his hometown. It took us a few hours of walking around Shamshabad to hand out all the flyers with a few ice cream stops. Haidrananda told me everybody wanted to know who the foreigner was. I was like a one-person parade. Everybody was staring. Haidrananda said he never had so much success handing out flyers. Everybody wanted to know if I was going to be there.

We got back to the temple in time to sit down for lunch. Govindananda started firing Haidrananda and me for handing out the flyers he told us to hand out instead of cleaning the temple. He asked me what I had been doing yesterday when the other three guys spent the whole day cleaning the temple. Truthfully, I was editing the QMP material. Govindananda told me the QMP material was NOTHING! The temple should come first. I could feel my button being pushed and the anger rising in me real fast. He went on to belittle me by asking who told me to work on the QMP material anyway. I confidently and truthfully told him that

Tathananda did and that he wants the finished material as soon as possible. Govindananda turned to Haidrananda and asked him, "Did anybody tell you to do the QMP material" Haidrananda didn't answer, but how could I work on a discourse in Tamil without a translator? Govindanada didn't think of that. Govindananda turned back to me and asked me who told me QMP was more important than the temple anyway. I interrupted him and told him, "I didn't decide one was more important than the other I just did the work I thought needed doing." In the end, we were all upset and finished our lunch in silence. I went and talked to Govindananda after lunch and asked him why it was wrong to hand out flyers. It was for Ugadi, just like all our cleanup is. He told me that three guys had to clean the whole temple themselves, and it took them all day yesterday. I told him to wait just a minute and went to talk to Naresh. Naresh had just hosed out the temple in about 30 minutes. Nobody had done anything more than that yesterday. I went back to Govindananda and told him what Naresh had told me, and Govindananda told me Suva told him about cleaning the temple all day yesterday. I threw up my hands and walked away in frustration. Suva had made up a story to make himself look good, and Govindananda assumed Suva meant all three boys. Something inside me just melted in the acceptance of the futility of making these people accountable. I was beyond caring about what these people thought happened or didn't happen. Did one of my buttons disappear?

My new job was to mop the temple. I found the bucket, filled it with water, picked up the mop, put it in the bucket, and started mopping. Nischelananda walked up to me like someone had just slapped him in the face, took the mop away from me, and started mopping. All I could do was laugh. I walked away amid a storm of comments in Tamil. The kid is a student in my English class and has been working with me for seven weeks now, and he still talks to me in Tamil like I understand. What could I do, fight for the mop? It was just too funny. If he wanted the mop that bad, he could have it. I found a broom and started sweeping the front steps. There are about forty steps, thirty feet wide with three landings about thirty feet long. It took a couple of hours. Just as I was finishing, Suva came and told me that Govindananda was calling. I'm still not comfortable with this method of summoning someone. I went up to his room. He directed me to sit in a chair and asked me if I was happy here. I didn't care anymore, I did my best to conform and be detached, but I just wasn't getting it. I told him, "No!," thinking that question was asked about eight months too late. He asked me if I had any of my own money. I told him I did. He got all flustered and started giving me a lecture about following the rules, and I interrupted him and told him it was the way Swami worked that made me choose to keep the money because I couldn't trust enough. Govindananda was getting upset now and said to me that it doesn't matter what the master does. It is all for our highest good. He went on to say that if he cut off both our legs, it would be because there was some spiritual reason for it. I told him I couldn't believe that and recounted my frustration with him, saying that he would take care of my visa, and in the end, I had to take care of it myself. Govindananda said that I missed a tremendous opportunity for growth by taking care of my visa myself. If I had let Swami, and I ended up in jail, it would have been for my highest good no matter how long I was in there or how bad the conditions were. Then Govindananda asked me what he could do to help me feel better about being in the ashram. My anger was building. I told him it was too late now! My ticket home was bought, and I was leaving on April 6. He thanked me for my honesty, interview over.

I was stunned at the man's blind faith. It might be OK for someone raised in this country with the spiritual training from a young age, but it was very different for me. I couldn't see how going to prison could possibly be for my highest good. Sure, there likely would have been lessons I could have learned in a foreign prison, but if nothing else life has taught me, teaching circumstances will present themselves as many times as it takes. I choose a less intense path.

Govindananda also talked about how I was a bad influence on Haidrananda because now he talks back. And how all the guys are talking about Haidrananda and me and about what I might be buying him when we go out together. Govindananda told me that Haidrananda was only my friend so that I would buy him things. He said poor village boys are like that. Haidrananda and I were friends before Hyderabad in Bidadi. We became friends when he was trying to teach me mantras, and he has his own money. He doesn't need me to buy anything for him. All Govindananda showed me was his own biased pre-conceptions. Govindananda did unintentionally tell me that my negative attitude got me sent to Hyderabad. I also found out during Govindananda's little tirade that you don't question anybody that is spiritually senior to you in the ashram. You don't ask questions. You don't talk about what was said. You just do it as if Swami himself told you. I understand this could be a beautiful opportunity to rise above one's ego. However, It sounds more like I have just admitted I am not ready for this type of command structure.

Love,

Karl

Chapter 26

Moving Your Awareness

Dear Lynn,

We were up till 1:00 am, making preparations for Ugadi. The traditional decoration is live neem tree leaves folded and tucked into a slit cut in the leaf and strung up like a Christmas garland, so the leaves all have to be fresh. In the morning, we did Guru Suva at 8:00 am, followed by me doing Arati. After almost an hour, Naresh did a Homa. It always takes Naresh a long time to get things together. Govindananda was getting pretty upset with all 12 people sitting waiting.

We handed out 5000 flyers, and only about 20 people were there by the time we were done. In the evening, there were probably 40 people, 15 being regular volunteers.

Govindananda made the traditional Ugadi prasad from ground coconut, scraped mango, a unique Indian sugar called jaggery that tastes and looks like brown sugar mixed with ginger and comes in a one-foot square cube. A potato peeler is used to shave the huge cube in preparation for cooking. The next ingredient is the petals of the neem flower for tartness. Tamerin is soaked for about one hour, so you get a lovely thick syrup, and finally two chili peppers are added. I am told it has all the flavors: sweet, sour, and bitter. We ate the syrup mixture with sweet rice. It sure is an interesting taste. One small spoonful was enough for me.

In the afternoon, a priest came to the temple and read what looked like the Indian equivalent of the Farmer's Almanac. All brahmacharis' attendance was compulsory. I was the only one there. Later, there was a volunteer meeting; all brahmacharis were required to attend. Once again, I was the only one there. Something is not right when I'm supposed to be the one with the attitude, but I am the only one attending meetings!

Tejananda and Suvananda almost came to blows over a misunderstanding this afternoon. Suvananda is a skinny little guy with a bad case of little man syndrome, and he has a gift for making people angry faster than anybody I know. He challenged the stocky farmer's kid, who could have easily knocked him out with one punch. Fortunately, Tejananda chose to walk away.

This evening I opened my book to read the following passage: UNTIL YOU HAVE FULFILLED ALL YOUR DESIRES, IT IS IMPOSSIBLE FOR YOU TO COME TO THE STATE OF CALMNESS, SERENITY, AND SELF-SURRENDER. When I first read this, I felt defeated, knowing I wouldn't achieve spiritual enlightenment in this life. However, upon deeper consideration, I realized it didn't mean to achieve all my desires first. It meant I needed to drop my desires to become enlightened. A desire is like a magnet. It pulls similar thoughts and circumstances to you, also known as the law of attraction. As long as you desire, you are attracting. Drop desire, and you rise above attachments to acceptance, bliss, and oneness with that which is formless. Dropping attachments sounds attainable, but it is my desire to drop the attachments that got me into this mess in the first place.

I was looking forward to some quiet time to finish editing the QMP material today. Haidrananda and I were just getting settled in when Suva came in and said something quickly in Tamil to Haidrananda and left before Haidrananda could respond. Haidrananda told me that Suva wants the computer for two days uninterrupted so he can lay out all his paperwork and do his accounting. Suva left on the scooter for a couple of hours, so we managed to translate a few pages. The first thing Suva did when he had the room to himself was hook up internet. Haidrananda, Virga, and I snuck in and checked the browser history and discovered he was shopping for a movie camera.

We walked into the village with the kids again tonight. Our little group was pretty quiet tonight. The village kids get all excited when they see me and rush into their houses and bring out mom and dad and then put their hands together and say Nithyanandam. If I say Nithyanandam back, they burst out in a big smile, and the parents give me the prayer salute. I get such a feeling of hopelessness for them. Mr. Negativity inside the temple is Mr. Popular outside the temple. By the time Tejananda had finished his call to his girlfriend, there were about a dozen people gathered in the narrow alleyway to have a look at the big white foreigner. Haidrananda told me that was the only reason they came. He says he has sat at that phone booth lots of times, and never has one kid come to see him, but every time I come, the crowds come out. I still can't get used to it. After sitting and waiting for Teja to finish talking with his girlfriend, we tease him by telling him to enjoy being able to speak now because soon it will only be, "Yes, dear. Yes, dear. Yes, dear." He gets embarrassed so easily.

I got my new bug screen installed today. It took all day to find the right guy with the right key to let me into the right room to get the rusty old tools. I have been skipping supper for the past few days. The village kids are taken home before serving supper. This means we don't eat until after 9:00 pm. which is only an issue when I get up at 4:30 am to dress the deities. And after the four-mile round-trip walk, my clothes are soaked and dirty from sweat and clouds of powdery road dust. All I want is a few scoops from a cool wash bucket. Even the water from the cold water tap is warm from being heated by the sun all day in the roof cistern.

I enjoy our walks through the village at night. I get to see into all the houses because of the heat; everything that will open is open. Most homes in this village have curtains for a door. Every place that I have seen is painted sky blue inside. Most have no furniture. The family sits on grass mats in the middle of the room on the concrete floor to watch TV. The TV looks so out of place in the little austere concrete houses. While the family is watching TV, the mom is outside cooking supper on a fire. Haidrananda tells me they do that when they can to save gas. Some people sit on a blanket thrown down on the dusty dirt street to get out of the hot concrete house that has been heated by the sun all day. Some bring their cots out and sleep in the street. Other homes have a little enclosed patio that becomes their temporary bedroom when it is so hot. When we walk by the people on their mats and cots, they often give me the prayer salute and say Nithyanandam. Even after all the guys have responded with Nithyanandam, the people keep saying it. Haidrananda told me they only want the big white foreigner to say Nithyanandam. So we tested Haidrananda's theory, and only I responded with Nithyanandam when the next couple of people said Nithyanandam, and sure enough, me saying Nithyanandam was enough. Maybe the villagers could see something in me I couldn't.

This book I am reading made a big deal about how an ideal spiritual householder is much more challenging to attain than being an ideal spiritual Sannyas who renounces everything. This message must be why I was given this book because I have no more inclination to read it. We watched a swami discourse on the Bhagavad Ghita in the temple basement that coincidentally said the same thing: you can pursue spiritual goals in the material world. After all, who would support all those begging Sannyas if not for householders?

This morning, Suva went off to get the cooking gas tank filled. The tank looks like a Western propane tank but painted red. Seeing Suva leave, Haidrananda and I went to use the computer room to continue translating the QMP material, but the door was locked with a new padlock. I don't get frustrated anymore. Finishing the QMP material is probably just more tapas (spiritual challenge).

When I asked Suva for the key to the computer room when he returned from getting gas, he got this wicked little grin on his face and said, "No, I need the computer all day today." His small-man complex was showing again. I might have to go into Shamshabad to send my weekly email home. Suva told Haidrananda he was mistaken about the dates and wouldn't let Haidrananda go into Hyderabad for another two weeks for his doctor's appointment. I was with Haidrananda at his last appointment and knew Haidrananda was right. Suva relishes the power to be able to say no to people. His appointment as head of this temple was, without a doubt, intentional tapas for all of us. We are all finding ourselves detaching from Suva and his unintentional nature.

Love,

Karl

Chapter 27

Snake! Snake! Snake!

Dear Lynn,

After evening Arati, Suva handed Haidrananda his missing English book with the excuse that he found it in the waste and saved it for him. The book was pristine, still brand new. It was never in any kitchen waste bucket. Suva confided in Haidrananda about how everybody was so mean to him here in Hyderabad. He was so happy in Bidadi when he had nothing to do. Here, it is too much. It sounds like Suva didn't choose his position as head of the ashram. He was being spiritually challenged like the rest of us.

Govindananda announced this morning at the breakfast table that he is leaving tomorrow for a month in Kenya. He told us that he got a few phone numbers from a participant in one of his intro talks a few months back. He pursued them, and now the Kenyans have arranged an intro talk for every evening of the month in Kenya plus an ASP every weekend. I felt like I should be more grateful for the experiences that challenge me and use those moments to dig deep and resolve my issues.

After noon, I finished my wash and was about to ask Suva to use the computer when I noticed him preparing the scooter to go out. I asked for the computer room key. He got the key and opened the door for me. I guess our little talk about working together helped, especially after Govindananda's announcement that he would be gone for a month. I reminded him of his promise this morning to finish his work before noon, and that locking the door was not working together. I understand that he feels his work is essential, but my QMP work is important to me also, and it would be better to share rather than fight over the computer. He promised to complete his work as soon as he could. It was time for all of us to listen to another episode of Bhagavad Ghita. Suva did his computer work while the rest of us watched Bhagavad Ghita. When the DVD was over, I checked on Suva. Now I understand why it takes six days for Suva to enter a month's worth of receipts into a spreadsheet. Receipts that nobody can see are spread all over the room (apparently in chronological order). He is typing with one finger into a spreadsheet. He doesn't know how to use formulas, so he is using a calculator to find totals. I suggested free online typing training, which just made him defensive. With new understanding, it was easier to detach and walk away.

This evening after supper, I was admiring the stars when I saw a shooting star. It was very clear and lasted for a full two seconds or so. I took it as a sign that I was making spiritual progress. Teja came around the corner and made hand gestures that indicated he saw it too. After Suva finally finished his record-keeping, Haidrananda and I got a few hours of computer time in. We were so close to finishing at 9:45 when the power browned out.

This evening, when we went into the village after supper with the kids, I absent-mindedly stepped into a hole in front of the corner store. The hole was about 18 inches around and as deep. I didn't hurt myself. A few people even rushed to grab me, but how could this be? It was a hole in a dirt road, kick some rocks in, put in a big stick to warn people, and the problem is solved. But no, you stand at the counter, make your purchase, turn around, and your first step is right into the hole. The shop keeper even sweeps the dirt around the hole instead of in it. What kind of insanity is that? I haven't seen a sidewalk yet that doesn't have some holes, slabs lifted out, or slabs missing. The sidewalk stone slabs are arranged to cover the filth in the ditch underneath. Sidewalk stones are displaced for many reasons. I saw one guy lift a slab out to retrieve his chicken because someone else left another slab out for his chicken to fall in. By the way, the slab removed to get the chicken out was not put back either. That slab may still be tipped up against the wall today. As a result, everybody gets the benefit of spiritual tapas in the form of holey sidewalks every time they go for a walk. You absolutely cannot go window shopping or daydream on these streets.

It never ceases to amaze me how persistent some people can be. Every morning during Guru Puja, there comes a point in the chanting when you place a flower on your head. Every morning, Suva puts the flower too far back on his head, and it falls off the back of his head. You would think after years of placing flowers on his head, he would have figured out how to keep a flower up there. That is persistence!

Suva was using the computer again. I told Govindananda I was going into Shamshabad to use the internet. He said, "Sure, go ahead." Haidrananda snuck out with me, but halfway out to the highway, he said he was getting fear. He made sure I got on the right bus and then went back. His premonition was correct because everybody was looking for him. The computer place was having trouble with their internet connection. Only one computer was connecting to the internet, and it was busy. I left to find another shop. The only two other computer places I could find were closed. I braved crossing the busy highway for ice cream. I am getting better at crossing busy streets now. I just start walking slowly across the road. The cars and trucks honk as they go around you. First, they go in front of you, and as you walk farther across the lane, they go behind you. The ice cream shop's freezer was having trouble working, so the ice cream was getting soft. What is it with power in this area? When I got back to the internet place, I got to use the lone internet computer. I got an email from my boss back in Canada telling me that he was looking forward to hearing all my stories. He also said he would continue to contact me through email to keep me up to date with what I needed to know to make my transition back to work easier. While I was replying to an email from Lynn, Haidrananda walked in with Suva right behind. Apparently, Suva needed two documents printed immediately for Govindananda to take to Africa, and Haidrananda knew where he could get them printed. The print job ended at about the same time I finished with the internet. Suva told Haidrananda to return on the scooter with him. Haidrananda told Suva that he would prefer to return with me. Suva told Haidrananda, "Karl came on his own; he can find his own way back."

How to build respect and work with people by Suva! All my attempts at diplomacy with Suva fell on deaf ears. I was sure that most people would eventually respond positively if you responded with kindness long enough. Suva proved to be the exception to that theory. When Haidrananda and I got back from Shamshabad, I went in to see Suva. I was shaking because I was so angry. Fortunately for him, he had left the computer room door open and was fast asleep on the bunk bed. I resisted images of tying him up while he slept and dragging him behind his scooter! I quietly took advantage of his altered state of consciousness and removed one of the three computer room keys from the ring in the door padlock on the desk.

Being at a loss about dealing with Suva, I decided to follow Suva's example and live his every-man-for-himself lifestyle; I refused to do Arati that night. Naresh came to remind me 10 minutes after Arati was supposed to start that I needed to get Arati prepared. I had to tell him three times before he finally understood that I wasn't doing Arati. Nobody said anything, not last night and not the next day.

This morning, I went into the computer room to get newspapers for English class, and the door was open! Nobody was inside. After English class, the door was locked. My pilfered key opened the door padlock so Haidrananda and I could continue working on QMP.

This morning, Suva came into the computer room while Haidrananda and I were just finishing up QMP. He didn't say anything about how I got into the locked computer room. He told us that he was going into the city to get some parcels and was taking Naresh and the grounds keeper. I shared that QMP would be finished soon, and I would need the internet to send it off to Tathananda. Suva told us we couldn't use the internet without his supervision. While we were waiting, we should clean out the Ananda Saba meeting room. We said, "Sure!"

to avoid any arguments. After Suva was gone, Haidrananda and I looked at each other and both said in unison, "It's already clean." It had been thoroughly washed out a few days earlier for Ugadi. We straightened the carpets and took away the dried up flowers left in front of Swami's picture. Why is this guy always pushing how far my patience can go? In retrospect, Suva was one of the best cosmic teachers of patience I have ever met.

There was big excitement this afternoon. Haidrananda started picking up washed pots from the sidewalk outside the kitchen to put them away and got hissed at by a big snake. He dropped the pots and ran faster than I have ever seen him move, yelling "Snake! Snake! Snake!" Everybody came to see, even some villagers who were close enough to hear. In the end, it was Teja, the farmboy, who got a ten-foot-long stick and beat it to death. Teja definitely got a little overzealous. We will need to replace a few smashed-in pots, and the washing stool is in worse shape than the snake. There was an electrical wire hanging about 6 feet above the sidewalk for lighting. It got whacked to the ground, but the snake is dead! While I am typing this journal entry, the boys are burning and saying mantras over the snake's dead body. It was about 5 feet long and as big around as a man's forearm. It was grey with large black circles on its back. They told me it was of the cobra family, but not poisonous. They assured me it was still plenty dangerous as it could wrap around your arm and break it.

Love,

Karl

Chapter 28

My Ticket Home

Dear Lynn,

I am sitting here in front of the fan playing Solitaire on the computer because this is the coolest place in the whole temple, and there is little else to do. I want to walk in to the village to get a cold drink, but by the time I get back, I will need three showers and a fresh set of clothes.

Suva must have returned very quietly to his room next to the computer room. I just happened to look up as he tried to slip away. I jumped up and asked him for the internet to be connected. He looked surprised but honored his agreement and unlocked the wire from the back door to his room and rerouted the wire into the back door of the computer room. It is a huge relief to get QMP finished and emailed off today. Now that the document is complete, I remembered a meditation Haidra and I wrote down from memory that I needed to transcribe more accurately. I have no reference for the meditation here at the temple. I'm sure people at the Bidadi Ashram will find the error and fix it. I also took advantage of the available time to get caught up on my email.

Tonight when I went to Arati, I found out that last night when I was upset with Suva and didn't do Arati, the guys covered for me. Suva never found out. With friends like that, how can I stay angry? I won't put my friends in that position again.

Nishcelananda was happy to get permission to go and renew his driver's license, until someone from Bidadi said no. Now Nischcel will have an expired license. An expired license is like no license at all. He will have to apply for a new license and pay all the fees and expenses for all the exams and road tests again for a new license. The morning before, Ugadi Haidrananda and I spent the morning handing out flyers. In the afternoon,

Haidrananda went to another village and did the same thing all over again. I was tired from one village this morning, and he did two villages with a back problem. He was lying down in pain in his room when Suva came in his room and told him he had promised to help decorate for Ugadi. Haidrananda acknowledged his promise, but now he is in pain and needs to rest. Instead of expressing compassion and working out an alternate arrangement, Suva immediately puffed out his chest, pulled out his cell phone, and called Bidadi about Haidrananda not being able to do his work because of a medical problem. He gave no explanation of all the work Haidrananda did leading up to the incident. Someone in Bidadi told Suva to call Haidrananda's family to pick him up and get him off the premises.

In the past, I enjoyed talks with Tathananda, sharing insights and frustrations, so I shared some tactful comments about temple life while he is away in my email, but his reply to my QMP email sounded like he was a completely different person. There was no conciliation or understanding, only ashram policy, which was to respect the position and its authority regardless of how I might feel about the decisions or the person holding that position. The email also told me not to use the computer for any reason until I talked to him or Govindananda. Playing games, even Solitaire, on an ashram computer was not appropriate.

Then I got another email within minutes, which stated that I must immediately return any money the ashram spent on my VISA. The ashram money only covered a small portion of my Sri Lankan VISA expenses. I saw this email to be a clear indication that my stay in India was over. I showed Suva the email, and he agreed I needed to return to the Bidadi Ashram and resolve this issue. Suva started the process of booking me a bus ticket to Bidadi. The process started with Suva fruitlessly trying to connect to Tathananda in Brazil. It took an hour and a half to contact Bidadi for confirmation. My ticket was booked for 7:00 pm that night.

These are the people who are in charge of the spiritual development of the people in their care. My ideas about how that looks day to day were utterly at odds with what I saw and felt here. I was disappointed that my confession about problems with my spiritual expectations was not recognized as an opportunity for some insight or solution from a more experienced ashramite. One of the few times I opened up for some spiritual insight and council, my trust was destroyed.

Preparations to return to Bidadi were a little unreal, like a dream come true to be able to walk away from this beautiful temple with the barbed wire fencing. I didn't want to pinch myself in case I woke up, and this was just a dream. I finished my packing and started saying my goodbyes. Suva took my backpack on the scooter to the highway for me. Haidrananda walked the 2km to the bus stop with me. We ended up waiting a half-hour for a bus, which means everybody else did too, so the bus was more than full by Western standards. Suva and I just pushed our way in, backpack and all. For some reason, Suva felt he needed to come with me and pay for the bus himself. One tour operator told me that all I had to do was wait in Shamshabad, and the bus would stop and pick me up on its way through to Bidadi, but Suva knew better. We got to Hyderabad at 6:30 pm. The cheaper bus was not available, so I was upgraded from a 350rs bus to a 400rs AC bus. I almost laughed out loud when I sat down in the bus seat and leaned back, and saw my AC unit above my head. It was a little electric fan. At this temperature, all it did was blow hot air in my face. I got much better cooling by opening the window. I just leaned my head against the window post and let the wind blow. I had to close my eyes every so often when a cloud of exhaust or dust hit my face. The bus spent the first couple of hours touring Hyderabad. The bus picked up a parcel here, a passenger there, and two ladies with their screaming little sweethearts at one point. They sat right behind me. I put in my earplugs! Finally, the bus pulled into a dark narrow side street where three Greyhound-sized buses were parallel parked. They were so big on this little street that no car could pass. We were transferred to one of the bigger buses. Thankfully, I got a front seat with the most legroom. Shortly after the bus got underway, the assistant bus driver started a musical movie. I tried to sleep for twelve grueling hours of trying to find a comfortable position in a seat where the headrest on the short seats supports your shoulder blades, and there is no room to recline. Sitting up straight and curling my legs half under the seat was the best I could do.

The bus got into Bangalore too early at 8:00 am for a caramel frappe at the coffee shop that didn't open until 10:00 am. They'd be out of business in Canada. I talked to 3 different conductors, and the consensus was bus 226M would get me to Bidadi. Forty-five minutes later, bus 226M took me to Bidadi, where a short auto-rickshaw trip finished the trip to the ashram office. I signed in right under Lynn's sign out just two minutes before to leave for Bangalore. Missing Lynn was disappointing! I started walking up to the kitchen to see if I could get some food, and I met a friend. As we began talking, Lynn came up to us and said she was going to Bangalore. Did I want to come? Lynn had signed out, but her auto-rickshaw had not arrived yet. She saw me get out and didn't get my attention until now. It was a much more relaxed trip back to Bangalore. Lynn and I took our time walking along Brigade Road. I finally got my caramel frappe and pizza. I even had a second caramel frappe before we returned to the ashram.

In the bunkhouse, all the bottom bunks were taken. The blessing is that the top bunk I chose was right under a ceiling fan. In addition to the cooling breeze, the wind keeps the mosquitos away. I put my earplugs in. I don't remember even turning over once. I didn't wake up until the guys came back in from Guru Puja at 8:00 am to change for breakfast, even with my feet hanging out the end of the too-short bed.

Love,
Karl

Chapter 29

A New Level of Detachment

Dear Mom,

I found the ashramite to get a locker from and got my passport and computer locked up. I have to fight my Western inclination to nest build and settle in with a better bed and better location in the dorm. Lynn and I talked to Priya today about paying back ashram money. She didn't know anything about having to pay back anything. It was a big relief to hear that I should forget about the money. The ashram was more concerned about what I might say about my ashram experience when I get back to Canada. She didn't want anybody to miss out on the opportunity to experience Swami just because I didn't have the experience I expected. I told her my thick-headedness was my issue. I would encourage people to make up their own minds. She seemed happy with that and said that I didn't need to worry about department work. I could just relax until I left in a few days. I felt a weight lift off my shoulders.

My priority was to wash my clothes from traveling. It is incredible how dirty one gets traveling in this country. It doesn't help when you wear white. I had just started washing when a female ashramite came up to me with a water tap in her hand, not only the handle but the whole faucet, to tell me that she broke the tap off and there was water everywhere in the women's washroom. I helped the plumber by standing at the door to redirect the women to the other washroom so the plumber could repair the tap. The job was completed in a half-hour. I just got back to doing my laundry, and the water cistern ran dry. I had to go to the pump house, turn the bore well pump on, and open the right valve to fill the water tank on the men's bunkhouse. The pump quit after 5 minutes. Now I had to find the electrician. The electrician was located and informed, and no waiting was required. Five minutes of pumping was enough water to finish my laundry. Keeping this ashram operating was part of the spiritual challenge.

The first night I slept in Bidadi, I was so tired I probably could have slept anywhere except on Hyderabad's overnight bus. Last night was a different story. I was dreaming about something that was causing my ear to tingle and itch uncontrollably. I half woke up in a cloud of mosquitos. I half-heartedly swatted them away until I realized how many there were. I slid down under the sheet, the way the Indian boys sleep. This morning's priority was to get a mosquito net. I found two heavy pieces of wire used to reinforce concrete brick walls, advantages of an ashram under construction, and bent them into two hoops like a Western-style wagon. I fastened them over the bed so my top half would be under the net. A trip to town always included filling my buddies' shopping lists. As I was walking toward the ashram exit, I asked my angels for an auto-rickshaw to show up. As I walked past the last building, an auto-rickshaw stopped right beside me. It was better than if

I had phoned and ordered it. There are definitely more synchronicities here at the ashram.

The tailor in Bidadi curiously seemed to understand what I wanted quickly. I wanted a flat piece of mosquito netting 2 meters by 2 meters square. I waited for my new mosquito net by walking a couple of blocks for ice cream, where I met my new lower bunkmate. We walked back to the tailor together so he could see my new mosquito net. While we were sitting and chatting, I realized there was an awful lot of material piled up beside the sewing machine. After quite a bit of discussion, he showed us that he was making a 2-meter cube. My $2.00 mosquito net was now $10.00. I was not happy, but what could I do?

My wire hoops were grossly undersized now. I pulled the hoops off and found an empty lower bunk. Just as I was enjoying my new netting and getting into a good meditation, my buddy interrupted and said he would help me move to another bunk. Apparently, the guy who hadn't slept there for a long time had been quarantined with a dozen others who had contracted measles. He was getting out of quarantine that day and would need his bunk back. I reluctantly moved back to the top bunk under the ceiling fan. It was the third bed in two days. I wired two half-inch plastic pipes wagon-style again to the bed, threw the huge net over the little pipes, and tucked in the rest.

I thought it was an April Fools' joke, but no, the music at 4:30 am kept playing loud! Somebody decided we should all get up at 4:30. The ashram was quiet and a little cooler that early in the morning. Returning from the washroom, I ran into the electrician who said, "Sorry for the disturbance." He had been asked to hook up the speakers in the dormitory because the brahmacharis were not attending morning Guru Puja at 7:00 am. Two and a half hours to get ready is a bit much. Most of them just went back to sleep.

As I walked up the hill to the temple, there was nobody on the ordinarily crowded road. The temple was equally deserted. The only person I saw was another Canadian stripping the lingam for fresh new clothing. We talked while he dressed the lingam before we went up to the banyan tree. We meditated until the scheduled meditation started. There were only a handful of people there. The 4:30 wakeup call didn't work.

After Guru Puja, Pierre and I had tea like in the old days. Well, I had horlicks, plus there were cookies for sale in the Galleria. What a great way to start the day!

There was a discourse on today called "Living with the Ananda Ghanda." I attended half out of interest and half out of boredom. I arrived early as usual. After sitting and waiting for quite a while, I went to the office to see if I needed to register, as all the other participants arriving had cards pinned to their chests. When I stepped into the office, it was full of people and our speaker, Rajananda, was chatting like he had nothing else to do. I went back into the Ananda Saba to continue waiting. Forty-five minutes later, Raja finally arrived. Shortly after Raja sat down, another ashramite squatted down beside me and quietly asked me to leave at

Raja's request as I hadn't attended the ASP test this morning. What could I say? It was true, and I left with a surprisingly detached feeling. After responding to a friend's email about his experience at Dhyanapeetam, the same ashramite came into the library and told me that after I left the discourse, Raja told the entire audience to leave if they did not write the test. The ashramite said after all the test skippers left, only a few people remained, so the surprised Raja changed his mind and allowed them to stay. Nobody came to get me! I felt like I should have been angry for being singled out, but there was no reaction, only peaceful detachment. My detachment was my lesson, showing me that despite not being able to levitate and transform lead into gold, I had changed. I had already attended the workshop before going to Hyderabad. I checked around; nobody here has heard of April Fools' Day!

It was a slow hot day—hot enough to cook eggs on the sidewalk. I couldn't walk around without my hat. Even the locals were hot! I went into Bidadi for some fresh fruit juice and ice cream. The oranges were wonderful, but try putting the orange in the microwave for about 20 seconds on high, and you will get some idea of how hot it was.

At the ashramite meeting this evening, Swami announced that all ashramites would attend four classes: GMA, QMP, acharya, and English. The lessons are just as important as the rest of the programs. If ashramites show dedication and hard work, they will be rewarded by being promoted to the inner circle of decision-makers. However, if they aren't dedicated, they will be shipped to another center. Too many people are not attending Guru Puja in the morning, so the rule of no sleep until you drop has been changed: be in bed by midnight. You must always take a bath before you go into the temple in the morning and at night. Attendance is handled by the department head when you report for department work each morning. All reports are collected daily and sent to Swami. All inner circle members are available for counseling between 5:00 am and midnight, and anything discussed in a counseling session will "not backfire on you." I wonder if my leaving after my confessions had anything to do with that rule? Department heads needed to be respected. All ashramites must ask permission before they can leave the ashram. Only if you have permission may you leave. You must sign the register in the office when you leave. The reality is that permission to leave is rarely granted. We are told it is for our own good. The official language of the ashram is English. Ironically, it was announced in Tamil and not translated. The last announcement was that there will be a suggestion box placed in the office. You are to put your suggestions in the box with solutions and how you will take responsibility for implementing the change. The last half hour of the meeting was in Tamil, with no translation provided.

After the meeting, it was 11:30 pm—time for a bucket bath. I finished washing my hair with my almost too-small bar of soap. I envisioned getting a new bar of soap when the soap popped out of my fingers, making a perfect arc right into the pooper hole despite all my juggling efforts to catch or deflect it. It didn't just do a belly flop into the hole, but a deep dive out of sight into the trap of the toilet. I know what you are thinking, but there is no lid to close on an Eastern toilet. The bar of soap was gone. It is not that I was afraid to put my hand in there. My hand was too big, as I discovered on a previous occasion. To get another bar of soap from my box of supplies under my bed, I had to dry off, get dressed and begin the navigation of the obstacles between the men's washrooms/toilets and the bunkhouse. The first obstacle is a three-foot-wide by four-foot deep ditch that the gurukul foundations are being constructed in. I successfully jumped the foundation ditches on both sides of the building site. Now I had to carefully walk around two large puddles of wet concrete in the dim light of a single light at the other end of the construction site. It is a simple task to walk across the bridge to the new extension to the Ananda Saba building from the wet concrete. There were only two uncovered pits here, a few sand and gravel piles, but lots of pipes sticking out of the floor for future electrical wires. I made my way carefully across the site with only dim moonlight to guide me to the opposite corner where I had stacked up a pile of cement blocks like stairs so I could step through a window opening. The blocks had been removed sometime today on the dark outside of the building by the plumbers digging ditches to lay piping. It was a combination of memory and intuition to remember where the packed earth was to step on without slipping into the ditches and not trip over the pipes and hoses haphazardly laying all over the place. The hoses have been patched by wrapping a rag around the leak. The rags keep the spray down, but the water turns freshly unearthed dirt into deep, sticky mud that cannot be tracked into any building. Navigation to the bunkhouse was successful this time. Now to find my bunk in the dark amongst the 40 or so other beds in the wide-open bunkhouse to dig the soap out of my precious supply of toiletries. Getting supplies of any kind from the ashram stores was always more hassle than hiring an auto-rickshaw and getting them myself from town. It takes longer to navigate to my bed from the washroom than it does to have my bucket bath.

With soap finally in hand, it was time to navigate the minefield of construction back to my wash bucket. At least the water in the rooftop cistern at night is warm after being heated by the sun all day.

Love,

Karl

Chapter 30

Western Expectations

Dear Mom,

This morning I took a chance and tried to jump the footings ditch in my lungi (man skirt). Midflight, my foot got caught up inside my lungi. I had visions of looking up from the bottom of the ditch at people gathering to see the big guy lying in the bottom of the ditch, but my foot, still tangled up in my lungi, landed on solid ground! I barely had enough inertia to carry me to the other side. What a relief. I don't think I'll ever get used to wearing a lungi, certainly not enough to wear it in Canada. Later in the morning, the electrician stopped by to visit. We both learned a lot about each other's cultures during our time working together, upgrading the ashram's power grid. His boss still calls me 6.5 ever since he found out I was 6'6" tall. As I was washing my dish this morning, some of the Indian ashramites stopped to tell me they would miss me. I politely smiled and thanked them, realizing in a few days, they would probably forget all about me until something we had done together would trigger a memory for a moment.

This afternoon, another Canadian and I went into Bidadi for an ice cream meditation. We went straight to the bakery/juice shop, where all the auto-rickshaw drivers hand out, and got a sweet lime juice. They just throw the limes in the blender with a scoop of sugar and some refrigerated water and blend for a minute. The concoction is poured into your glass through a strainer. It is pure goodness. Then we carefully picked our way around turned-up sidewalk stones, too many auto-rickshaws parked too close together, and all the other people trying to navigate the same obstacles to get to the ice cream shop. We had a little cup of ice cream with a flat wooden spoon that seemed to be the normal portion here, which just wasn't enough today. My buddy had another, and I found a guy who sold me a half liter tub of double chocolate. In this 100 degrees heat, it was heavenly. We took the time to walk all the entire four blocks to the end of the commercial street. There was a small shop that sold the traditional Western frozen chocolate milk treats. This owner gave us his own frozen concoction. It looked like pale frozen chocolate milk but tasted like frozen milk flavored with cardamon and blended cashews. I loved it. It was his own chai-flavored treat! We walked back to the first shop again, where we got more frozen treats, and I got a liter of cold water in a plastic bag. Even cold water is a treat on an ashram without refrigeration.

As we continued down the street, we noticed a "medical center," or drug store in the West, that we had to explore. You could buy band-aids that these people called sticky plasters. Everything a Western drug store would have was there efficiently packed into about a tenth of the space. There was even a tube of ointment called "Krack." The developers obviously had no idea of their product's alternate Western meaning. The product advertised it would soften the thick dried and cracking skin on the sides of your heels from walking barefoot. I just used a laundry scrub brush in my bucket bath to brush off the softened dead skin.

This evening, I went up to Lynn's window in the women's dorm and showed her the Krack box. While we were having a good chuckle, an ashramite saw me and told me I could not go up to a woman's window because I could see all the dorm inside from that window. Actually, Lynn and another ashramite both had their bunks enshrouded in blankets so that I couldn't see anything outside the small space between their two beds, but his error did prove that he had never looked in the window.

While I was squatted down at my locker in the dark, putting away my tube of Krack, Rajananda stole in and lay down in his bed. Obviously, he didn't see me because laying down before midnight was forbidden. Rajananda would often come into the bunkhouse to check that the beds were empty. The message of the yelling and screaming in Tamil was clear. Body language is the same, no matter the language. As a matter of fact, the ashramite who normally does Guru Puja in the morning and Arati at night disappeared this afternoon. Someone else was doing Arati this evening. Rajananda said he would send slackers away. I will have to find out if the rumors are true.

I am enjoying these last few detached days back in Bidadi before returning to Canada. I am no longer vested in the outcomes of my studies and complying with arbitrary rules. The rules are meant to overwhelm our egos enough to force our issues to the surface for us to recognize/acknowledge and detach from them, thereby creating mental space to let bliss well up in its space. I admire the ashramites' determination to take each hurdle this organization throws at them and see it as an opportunity for growth. For me, the curtain has been pulled back to show me that any stress or frustration can lead to spiritual epiphany, no matter where you are or who you are with. The difference between epiphany and anger is one's perspective and capacity for detachment and reflection. I am forever thankful for the depth of my experiences at this ashram. I would never have gotten to experience the bliss I have in as short a time if I would have fumbled around on my own.

This morning's Guru Puja and Nithya Dhyan meditation didn't have the mystic, focus-harder-and-you'll-get-it aura about them. There was no more doubt in my heart. The anticipation and hope that I could move into a space of enlightenment were gone. I was already there. I understood with all my heart that I had arrived. This feeling of deep acceptance and peace was confirmation that the door to leave was open, not because I had finally passed some cosmic test, but because I realized that I was born with everything I needed to wake up and let the bliss pour in.

Last night, coming back from my bucket bath, I understood that in some small way, Swami has learned from my other Western seekers and me. I can't imagine how much of a challenge it must be for Swami to address our unique Western challenges with Eastern methods, but then that challenge may have been what the ashramites needed. Despite how similar we are, some fundamental differences made this experience blissfully unforgettable.

Packing to leave, there were a lot of mixed feelings. It wasn't until we were all done and the taxi had arrived that Priya told me I had to surrender my kavi. I was surprised to be so emotionally attached to this symbol of my journey, and I didn't want to leave it behind. I took my kavi off and handed it to Priya. She jumped back and told me she couldn't touch it. Our spiritual head had to receive it. Off to find Rajananda. I found him in the publishing room, talking via Skype with Swami in Los Angeles. After questioning, Swami Raja told me I had to take my kavi to the temple deities and place it at their feet, prostrate myself and say whatever words I felt I needed to say. So with the cab driver and friends waiting, I went up to the life-sized brass deity of Swami and put my kavi on his right foot. His left leg was crossed, so his left foot was in his lap, with Devi sitting on his left knee. I thanked the deity for sharing his ashram with me and all the experiences we shared. Almost in response, there was an internal torrent of images and feelings chronicling the past nine months faster than I could ever assemble myself, yet barely within my ability to recognize and acknowledge. I was so surprised I didn't realize I was experiencing a beautifully bliss-filled moment of no thoughts until my thoughts and judgments all came rushing back in.

My experience here was now complete. As I retrieved my kavi from the deity's foot and started my walk back down the hill, I could feel the intense energy in my head, like the dizziness from getting up too fast from lying down. Something powerful happened between the deity and me. It felt like a cosmic hug goodbye, my final darshan. When I returned to Raja, he again refused to take the kavi. He told me he couldn't touch it. He had me place it on the table under Swami's picture. We exchanged niceties, and I made my way back to my small gathering of our friends to say our final goodbyes.

Riding away in our taxi to Bangalore was a huge relief and disappointment. Relief about finally leaving the challenging life at the ashram and disappointment that enlightenment wasn't some lightning bolt of revelation. Enlightenment, for me, is an ongoing process of increasing awareness of how my habitual responses manifest themselves. It is an awareness that happens easier with the tools and experiences learned from Swami. There is no doubt I feel lighter and less defensive now. I have had a few experiences in the past of bliss so intense you just want to sit down, close your eyes, and lose yourself in the expansive feelings. Now the bliss happens regularly. The most random things trigger my bliss now. It could be catching a glimpse of a bird landing in a tree out of the corner of my eye and falling in love with the beauty of nature or catching a few words of someone else's conversation as you pass them, remembering how you felt when you shared stories like that with someone in the past. The more often I get those blissful feelings, the more enlightened I feel.

It took the taxi driver in Bangalore quite a while to find the hotel recommended by a good friend at the ashram. When the driver finally did find it, we were not disappointed. It felt like heaven in the middle of the hot season walking into an air-conditioned room after trying so hard to find any place that was a few degrees cooler at the ashram. We quickly settled into our room, lowering our body temperature a couple of degrees closer to normal before going out to Brigade Street for a caramel frappe. There were no curfews and nobody to check in with. I felt like an adult again. We took our time and window shopped all the way down the street. After a great pizza, we looked at new glasses for Lynn, which were not the bargain we were led to believe they would be, so we didn't get them. We bought a travel book about Australia and generally just enjoyed the freedom to do what we wanted when we wanted. That evening, the hotel manager called us to tell us there had been a mix-up in our reservation. We did not have a reservation. He would meet us at breakfast. How to keep customers in suspense! The mix-up turned out to be another guest had registered with the same name, so the hotel assumed we were the same person. What are the odds of that happening in a little out-of-the-way hotel in Bangalore? We re-registered after breakfast and got "shifted" to another room. We went from a view of a solid concrete wall 6" outside our window to the second floor and a much larger expanse of bare concrete wall 10' away! Otherwise, the rooms were identical. The air conditioning worked, which was the most important thing.

A few days of sleeping in and all memories of spiritual tunes blasting at 4:30 am to get up for yoga all but disappeared. Shopping and being a tourist was enough of a challenge for the few days before leaving the country. One of those days, the rickshaw we were riding in pulled up beside another taxi. A good friend of ours from the ashram was in that other taxi in the middle of Bangalore traffic. We knocked on his window and scared him. It was an amazing coincidence that in all of Bangalore, we ended up side by side at the same traffic light. We enjoyed a good visit back at the hotel despite his busy schedule. This random meeting was more than a coincidence. The Universe was clearly showing us that ashram or no ashram, it wasn't finished with us yet.

Love,

Karl

Epilogue

Enlightenment Is a Subtle Process

My decision to travel to India had no preconception about what might happen or what would trigger the end of my time with my guru in India. I was naively open to the possibility that I might never come back to Canada. The reality of living on a new ashram under construction was nothing like I could have imagined. I imagined endless meditations and profound truths shared by an enlightened guru. The reality was more like trying to see my guru through a fog of my habitual responses. My guru shared many profound experiences and practices with me. If only I were open and sincere enough, he probably could have easily enlightened me. My guru told me an enlightened master can easily place his hand on you and instantly enlighten you, but if you are not ready, the abrupt frequency change would likely only last a few moments before your ego took over again. There is another significant caveat to attaining enlightenment, and that is the acknowledgment of the choices you made before you incarnated into your present form. If for some reason, you chose not to be enlightened in this lifetime or at another time during this life, your guru will be able to read your choices in your Akashic records and respect your choice, even if you are not aware of that choice. Your guru can still teach you many life-altering skills and help you in profound ways, but it is up to you to let the magic in.

My time in India was undeniably beneficial, but I never got the earth-shaking, perspective-altering moment of divine awakening I always envisioned enlightenment to be. Spiritually, I had some profound experiences that collectively changed the way I deal with life's challenges. One of my first changes was my enhanced ability to drop into meditation and calm my mind. I could fall into meditation just about anywhere I could close my eyes and relax for a moment. Meditation was no longer an effort. I looked forward to meditation's enhanced energy and often meditated multiple times a day, even if just for a few moments. Another change was a distinct inner core of bliss-filled calmness, which often manifested itself while experiencing something in my life that, in the past, would have brought up feelings of anger or frustration, like driving. I had been an aggressive, intolerant driver. Now I am aware of the energies the moment they arise, before they become aggressiveness and intolerance, and I experience them as the pure undefined energy they are before I label them and enjoy the experience of the beautiful raw blissful energy. I revel in my new superpower. Meditation has given me the space and time to make a better choice instead of reacting out of habit. I am not always as mindful as I would like, but practice . . . .

I continue to meditate daily and distinctly feel something is missing if I don't. I am more in sync with the world around me in the form of intuitive nudges or synchronicities. The more I respond to the nudges and acknowledge them, the more they show up. Like when I get the urge to drive slower just before a police car drives by or little things like leaving the house in the morning and the feeling something is missing hits me. A quick check of my pockets usually reveals what I need to go back for. The nudges are just as strong to make another choice when I think about buying unhealthy food.

Recently, I found myself in a frustrating situation at work. I was intensely focused on the source of my frustration, imagining different ways to resolve the problem. Still, there was also a part of me that was sitting back chuckling about the fact that I chose to be frustrated when I could just as easily choose a different perspective and continue to be detached and relaxed. The moment I realized I was responsible for my choice to be frustrated, I said something unrepeatable more because of habit than the frustration at hand. The *Ah-ha!* was the emptiness and insincerity of the profanity. Instead of releasing pent-up frustration and anger, they were just hollow words without emotion.

Also new in my life is a better understanding of the mysteries of why things happen in my life and recognizing connections that I would never have previously. Connections such as meeting an old friend when I walked onto a job site looking for a summer job in a new town. Or understanding that choices I make for my highest good are rewarded with more synchronicities to facilitate that choice or not if I should make another choice. My life has become less mysterious and more predictable the more aware I become. Knowing some of the answers to my life's purpose creates more space for bliss and less frustration trying to understand. The path intuition/synchronicity leads me is not always clear at the time, but it is most often for my highest good. Requesting help from my guardian angels is almost always answered rarely the way I expect. For example, I once owned a large, rusty, old SUV that was expensive to operate and maintain, so I sincerely requested of my angels that someone rear-end my SUV in a way that the damage would not be my fault and whoever hit me would do it by their own choice on some level. The next day, I backed into a power pole while parallel parking and wiped out my passenger side rear bumper, tail light, and fender. That was not what I had in mind. I was half-laughing at being so promptly answered and half-accepting that the Universe had a much different perspective of what my intention was. Later that same day, I was backing into a tight parking space, and I hit a short steel parking bollard that wiped out the rear driver's side bumper, tail light, and fender. My rear-end collision was now complete, granted by my angels precisely as I requested. Unfortunately, the damage did nothing to help me get a more economical vehicle. In hindsight, I should have just requested the vehicle I wanted. Guardian angel requests are quicker and more successful the more creative freedom you give them. Understanding more of the reasons for what happens in my life and exerting some control is the biggest blessing I received from my time in India.

Enlightenment, for me, is not a switch that drops the dimensional veil and reveals a vast library of Universal truths and the wisdom to live them. Enlightenment is a gradually expanding process of subtle experiences and inner awakenings that profoundly raise awareness. In the words of my guru, it "makes life more juicy." The cumulative effect of all my awakening experiences and subtle energy shifts is more and longer moments of bliss.

Glossary

Ashram. A community of devotees that come together to learn from a spiritually enlightened person. The community supports the master and facilitates the expansion of his mission.

Ashramite. A person who lives and works on an Ashram in exchange for the lessons and learning he gets from the resident master.

Enlightenment. To understand how we are influenced by our parents, peers and society and overcome that influence.

Darshan. An energetic sharing of energy from someone accomplished enough in their own mastery. The result is an energetic entanglement that lifts your energy frequency a little closer to the masters energy level. Darshan may be accomplished by the touch of a master or the sight of some spiritually holy artifact or statue.

Deity. A brass statue of a spiritually significant person imbued by reverence and adoration with powers of love and oneness that will metaphysically inspire the beholder to become closer to the Prime Creator.

Dhoti. Piece of cloth worn by men wrapped around the waist extending to the ground.

Homa. A fire ceremony where aromatic spices and all worldly enticements are burned as an offering for the gods to use to manifest a form that can be viewed by devotees. It is common for a devotee to tell you that if you did not see a manifestation in the smoke that your devotion was not intense and pure enough.

Karma. On one level Karma can be a scale of justice; a person who commits a criminal act must balance that crime with a benevolent act. Spiritually, Karma can mean the balancing of a lifetime of being a ruthless sociopathic narcissist with a lifetime as a humble saintly philanthropist.

Kurta. Loose collarless shirt.

Mantra. Something repeated over and over again either out loud or internally as a tool to exert a degree of control over the run-away thoughts of our ego.

Meditation. Sitting peacefully in a quiet contemplative way. At the same time being mindful of your thoughts but not caught up in them. Watching your float by in your mind's eye without getting caught up in them.

Nithya Dyaan Meditation. A good introductory guided meditation used at this ashram. The most current version can be found at http://nithyanandatimes.org/nithya-dhyaan/.

Puja. At this ashram, it is the ceremonial chanting of mantras while undressing a large brass deity, washing the deity by pouring turmeric, milk and blessed water over a large brass deity, and finally redressing the deity.

Swami. Someone who has mastered the ability to detach from their ego and the habitual responses life triggers. Consequently a Swami Is not limited by beliefs and dogma.

Synchronicity. The seeming coincidental occurance of unrelated events that make you question how much influence you have over your reality.

Yogi. To live without the confines we impose on our selves, our habitual responses and judgments.

Manufactured by Amazon.ca
Bolton, ON